PIRATES IN PARADISE

NIAS – Nordic Institute of Asian Studies
STUDIES IN CONTEMPORARY ASIAN HISTORY
Series Editor: Robert Cribb, Australian National University

Indonesian Politics in Crisis
The Long Fall of Suharto 1996–98
Stefan Eklöf

The Indonesian Miltary After the New Order
Sukardi Rinakit

Power and Political Culture in Suharto's Indonesia
The Indonesian Democratic Party (PDI) and Decline of the New Order 1986–98
Stefan Eklöf

The Thaksinization of Thailand
Duncan McCargo and Ukrist Pathmanand

Thaksin – The Business of Politics in Thailand
Pasuk Phongpaichit and Chris Baker

Pirates in Paradise
A Modern History of Southeast Asia's Maritime Marauders
Stefan Eklöf

PIRATES IN PARADISE

A Modern History of Southeast Asia's Maritime Marauders

Stefan Eklöf

First published in 2006 by NIAS Press
NIAS – Nordic Institute of Asian Studies
Leifsgade 33, DK–2300 Copenhagen S, Denmark
Tel: (+45) 3532 9501 • Fax: (+45) 3532 9549
E–mail: books@nias.ku.dk • Website: www.niaspress.dk

British Library Cataloguing in Publication Data
Eklöf, Stefan
Pirates in paradise : a modern history of Southeast Asia's maritime marauders. - (Studies in contemporary Asian history ; 6)
1.Pirates - Asia, Southeastern - History
I.Title
364.1'64

ISBN 87-91114-36-6 (cloth)
ISBN 87-91114-37-3 (paper)

Typesetting by NIAS Press
Produced by SRM Production Berhad Sdn
Printed and bound in Malaysia

Contents

Illustrations

Figures

Maps

Preface and Acknowledgements

RESEARCH FOR THE THIS BOOK was carried out as part of a postdoctoral fellowship that I held at the Centre for East and Southeast Asian Studies at Lund University between September 2003 and August 2005. Above all, and apart from providing me with a dynamic and stimulating research environment at the Centre, the fellowship gave me the time to conduct in-depth research into the topic of contemporary piracy in maritime Southeast Asia. The Lund Asia Library also provided excellent facilities for conducting the research, and their dedicated staff did everything to provide me with any type of material that I required for the study.

The first phase of the project was undertaken during a visiting fellowship at the Nordic Institute of Asian Studies (NIAS) in Copenhagen from October 2002 to August 2003, which was made possible by a grant from Nordisk Forskerutdanningsakademi (NorFA). Like the Centre in Lund, NIAS also provided a stimulating research environment and excellent library facilities and support. Together with the Centre in Lund, NIAS also financed a workshop on Piracy and Non-Traditional Threats to Maritime Security, which I coordinated in May 2004, and which proved to be of great value for the project, especially because of the international contacts it generated.

I also wish to thank Crafoordska stiftelsen, Fil dr Uno Otterstedts fond för främjande av vetenskaplig undervisning och forskning, Stiftelsen Bokelunds resestipendiefond and the Swedish School of Advanced Asia-Pacific Studies (SSAAPS) for generous contributions to travel and other expenses in relation to the project.

Gothenburg, April 2006

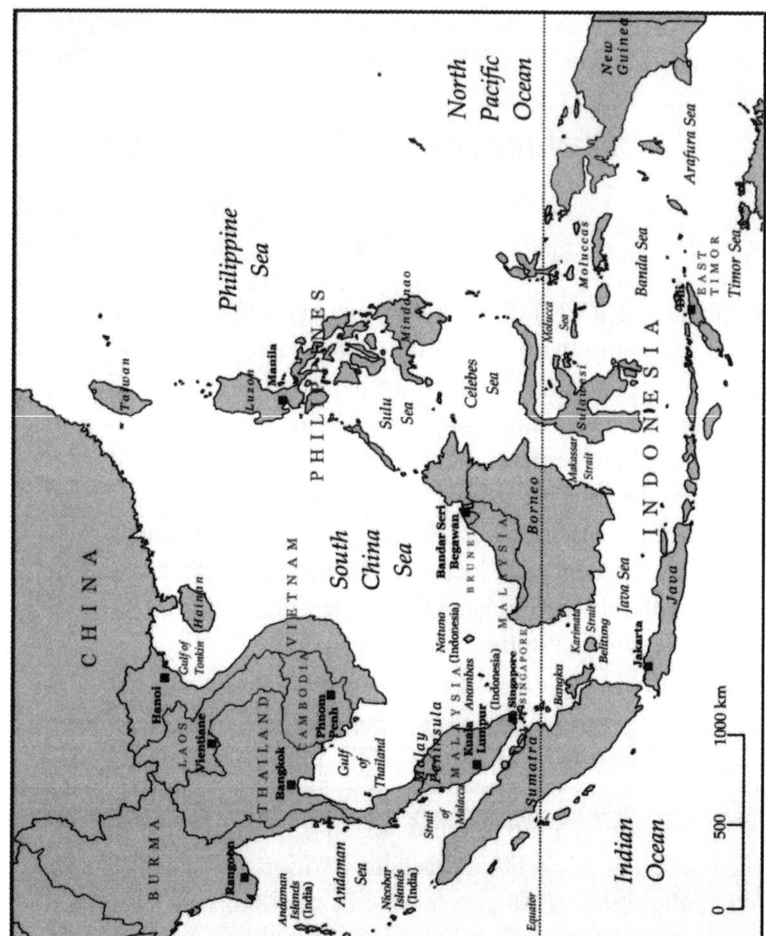

Map 1: Southeast Asia

CHAPTER 1

Introduction

FEW CRIMES IN HISTORY evoke as many colourful, and even romantic, associations as piracy. At least in Western popular culture, pirates, whether based on historical figures or purely fictional characters, seem to hold special fascination, not only for children but also for many adults. Who has not, for example, heard of the exploits and adventures of Henry Morgan, Captain Kidd, Edward Teach (alias Blackbeard) and Bartholomew Roberts, to mention only a few of the most prominent pirates of the 'golden age' of European and Atlantic piracy in the seventeenth and early eighteenth centuries? Depicted invariably as brave, adventurous, cruel, bloodthirsty and hungry for gold and treasures, the pirates of the golden age have in one way or another stood as models for numerous fictional characters in adolescent and children's stories like R. L. Stevenson's *Treasure Island* and J. M. Barrie's *Peter Pan*, as well as in action and adventure movies, especially in the 1950s but also more recently for instance in the blockbuster film, *Pirates of the Caribbean: The Curse of the Black Pearl*, released in 2003 and to be continued in a sequel due in 2006.

For all their diversity and creative imagination, the novels and movies have one thing in common: they were all produced long after piracy ceased to be a threat to maritime traffic in the Atlantic. During the last wave of Atlantic piracy between 1716 and 1726 – the days of Blackbeard and Roberts – there were probably few seafarers who would think of pirates as romantic figures, and the major contemporary account on the subject, Captain Charles Johnson's *General History of the Pyrates*, first published in 1724, is abundant with tales of arbitrary and often repellent violence by the pirates. In those days the Jolly Roger, the feared black or blood-red pirate flag generally featuring a skull or skeleton, fulfilled its purpose of persuading the crews of the target ships to surrender rather than die at the hands of the pirates.

Today's pirates rarely hoist the Jolly Roger, but just like their seventeenth- and eighteenth-century counterparts they strike fear in the hearts and minds of seafarers around the world. Many of them, moreover, are just as brutal as Blackbeard and his contemporaries, and over the past decade, at least hundreds, and probably thousands, of sailors, fishermen and other seafarers have been killed by pirates and maritime terrorists.

Pirates still roam the Caribbean, but in numbers the region is dwarfed by Southeast Asia, which currently accounts for close to half of all reported attacks world-wide. Pirate attacks actually seem to be more frequent in Southeast Asia today than they ever were during the golden age of Atlantic piracy. Historian Marcus Rediker has estimated that between 1716 and 1726, pirates captured and plundered an estimated 2,400 vessels, or an average of 218 per year. Between 2000 and 2004, by comparison, the International Maritime Bureau (IMB), which is the main source of information about contemporary piracy, recorded 920 attacks in Southeast Asia (out of a total of 1,944 world-wide), or an average of 184 per year. The IMB, however, believes that its figures only represent about half of the actual number of attacks, giving a total average of some 368 attacks per year in the region.[1]

This book sets out to describe the extent, distribution and character of piracy in Southeast Asia during the last 25 years and, above all, to explain *why* piracy, as it seems, has returned after having been all but extinct in the region – as in most of the rest of the world – for close to a century. Over the past decade, academics, journalists and various experts in maritime law enforcement have produced a stream of books and articles on the subject, citing a wide range of explanations for the recent resurgence of piracy, including economic, social, political and cultural factors.[2] As Ger Teitler has pointed out, however, most people interested in contemporary piracy have a 'legal, economic or police background, or have their roots in the world of insurance, security, ship owners or seafarer' unions' and tend to see piracy from a 'restricted, professional angle'.[3] Consequently, few analysts have hitherto attempted to look at the problem from a historical or comparative angle or otherwise tried to gain a more comprehensive understanding of the problem against the background of the current social, political and economic developments in the region.

Writing a contemporary history of a criminal activity is inevitably charged with problems of how to gain adequate and sufficient empirical information. Whereas quantitative data, such as statistical information about pirate attacks, are available, they only reflect part of the reality since many, if not most, attacks are never reported. Qualitative information, on the other hand, is scarce and largely anecdotal. Not only are the perpetrators of pirate attacks, for natural reasons, generally unwilling to share information about their activities but so too are many victims – for various reasons, including fears of reprisals and costly delays in connection with police investigations – unwilling to speak about their encounters with pirates. Moreover, since the issue under study is contemporary, most of the information that might be found in the archives of various law enforcement and investigating authorities, such as the police, navies and coastguards of the states involved, is classified or for other reasons inaccessible to the historian.

Whereas these circumstances are obstacles that need to be considered, they are by no means reasons for abandoning, or even suspending, the attempt to write a history of contemporary Southeast Asian piracy. A comprehensive – if perhaps not definite – account can be pieced together from what available evidence there is, including statistical data, narrations of reported attacks, the records of international bodies such as the International Maritime Organization (IMO) and testimonies in local and international media, and supplemented with interview material. Based on these, often piecemeal, sources, the task of the contemporary historian is to compare, combine and critically evaluate the evidence, and to interpret the sources against the background of a broad knowledge of the historical, political, economic, social and cultural context of the region as well as of the global processes affecting it. The result, it is hoped, is an account that not only describes the phenomenon and the different forms it has taken in Southeast Asia over the past decades, but also helps to explain its background and causes, and to understand it from a historical, local as well as global, and comparative perspective.

Notes

1 For the number of attacks between 1716 and 1726, see Rediker (2004: 33), and for the 2000–2004 figures, see ICC – International Maritime Bureau (2005a: 4). The figures here include attacks in and around Vietnamese waters, which the IMB does not include in its definition of Southeast Asia. As we shall see, however, the IMB's numbers are probably underestimations even if doubled.

2 See Eklöf (forthcoming) for a critical discussion of the main explanations cited in the literature.

3 Teitler (2002: 68).

CHAPTER 2

Piracy in Asian and World History

IN TERMS OF GEOGRAPHY, few other regions in the world seem as favourable for piratical activity as maritime Southeast Asia.[1] The region hosts the world's largest archipelago comprising Indonesia, Malaysia and the Philippines, with altogether over 20,000 islands and a combined coastline equivalent to several times the length of the equator. Many of the islands are uninhabited and have irregular and densely vegetated coastlines, secluded bays and navigable rivers, all of which provide pirates with numerous places to hide.

Since the dawn of history, maritime Southeast Asia has been a crossroad for maritime long-distance trade, and pirates have probably never been short of wealth-laden prey to choose from. In several places, such as the Straits of Malacca and Singapore, the long-distance trade passed – and still passes – close to the coasts and islands that provided the pirates of the region with suitable land bases from where to launch their attacks. The first historical reference to piracy in the region is from the early fifth century, when the Chinese Buddhist monk Faxian (Fa-hsien) wrote about the passage from Ceylon to Java that the 'sea is infested with pirates, to meet whom is death'.[2]

Whereas the pirates whom Faxian referred to probably consisted of relatively small, local groups, piracy was also linked to politics in pre-modern Southeast Asia, and the ability to control and channel piratical forces was a crucial element in the accumulation of political power. The maritime trading-state Srivijaya, which dominated the Strait of Malacca from the eighth century to around A.D. 1000, prospered, on the one hand, on its ability to provide protection for traders against pirates in the area and, on the other hand, on alliances with the region's semi-piratical sea nomads, *orang laut*, whose fast vessels forced merchant ships to call at the port of Srivijaya and pay tribute to its ruler.[3] Traders generally seem to have preferred these coercive practices to the threat of pirates outside of Srivijaya's control, and sources from the period speak of the fears that sailors had for the pirates who inhabited those parts of the southern Malacca Strait that were outside the control of the trading empire.[4]

In general, piracy in pre-modern Southeast Asia seems to have increased in times of declining state authority, such as after the decline of Srivijaya. Piratical activity could then take the form of well-planned and large-scale ventures, as testified by a fourteenth-century Chinese chronicler who wrote about the Malacca Strait area:

> The inhabitants are addicted to piracy [...] when junks sail to the Western [Indian] Ocean the local barbarians allow them to pass unmolested but when on their return the junks reach *Chi-li-men* [the Karimun islands] the sailors prepare their armour and padded screens as a protection against arrows for, of a certainty, some two or three hundred pirate praus [boats] will put out to attack them for several days. Sometimes [the junks] are fortunate enough to escape with a favourable wind; otherwise the crews are butchered and the merchandise made off with in quick time.[5]

In the fifteenth century, piracy was again relatively efficiently controlled in the Malacca Strait as the trading emporium of Melaka, based on the west coast of the Malay Peninsula, rose to power. Just as Srivijaya 500 years earlier, Melaka's naval power depended on alliances with the *orang laut*, and traders were attracted to the port city by its provision of protection and facilities for traders.[6]

This period of relatively safe conditions for maritime trade came to an abrupt end as the Portuguese established themselves in the region in the early sixteenth century and conquered Melaka in 1511.

In the sixteenth century, Portugul's maritime empire centred on the Indian Ocean stretched from Zanzibar on the east coast of Africa to the 'Spice Islands' of the Moluccas in eastern Indonesia. This was based on the supreme naval power the Portuguese enjoyed through their small and easily manoeuvrable vessels armed with cannons and muskets. Rather than promoting law and order on the high seas, however, the Portuguese attacked and sank the vessels of the Muslim traders who had dominated the Indian Ocean trading network up until the turn of the sixteenth century. They also issued certificates of safe conduct, *cartaze*, which local merchants were forced to buy in order to avoid being attacked by Portuguese ships. The Catholic missionary Francis Xavier sarcastically summarised the nature of the Portuguese *Estado da India* when he claimed that the learning of the Portuguese in the Moluccas was limited to the Latin verb *rapio* – 'I seize'.[7]

Even though there was, at least in theory, a consensus in Europe since antiquity that pirates should be considered as *hostis humani generis* – enemies of all mankind – the attitude towards piratical activity in practice was more ambivalent. Medieval jurists recognised the term 'piracy' and regarded it as an illegitimate activity, but the distinction between piracy and peaceful commerce was blurred and characterised, in the words of the British naval historian N. A. M. Rodger, by a 'very wide area of debatable ground and questionable practices'.[8] The ocean was basically an unregulated area where there was not much law and order even in times of peace, and privateering – essentially piracy sanctioned by the state – was an important instrument of war since few of the principalities and nascent nation-states in Europe at the time could afford to equip and maintain large regular naval forces. Issuing 'letters of marque' to private shipowners, which allowed them to attack and plunder enemy vessels for private gain, thus considerably expanded the naval capacity of England, France, the Netherlands and other European powers in the sixteenth, seventeenth and eighteenth centuries. In the mercantilist ideology of the age, moreover, trade and war were both seen as means towards the goal of national advancement at the expense of other nations, and state-sponsored piracy or privateering could thus, in analogy with Clausewitz's characterisation of war as an extension of diplomacy by other means, be seen as trade by other means.

An unintended consequence of the practice of privateering, however, was that it encouraged unregulated piratical activity as many of the privateers were unwilling to demobilise in peacetime. The irregular navies of the different European states, moreover, lacked the capacity to uphold law and order on the sea whether in times of war or peace. Privateers tended not to defend the merchant fleets of their own countries – the vessels of which were expected to be sufficiently armed to defend themselves – but to attack enemy merchant vessels and take prizes, thus doing little to clear the oceans from the 'enemies of mankind'.[9]

It was only when, in the spirit of Adam Smith and David Hume, mercantilism gave way to the encouragement of free international trade in the late eighteenth and early nineteenth centuries that the European powers and the United States began in earnest to combat piracy even outside their own territorial waters. As global trade, dominated by the North Atlantic powers, expanded around the world, European and American naval forces increasingly came to take on the task of policing the oceans and shipping lanes against piratical activity regardless of where they occurred. Since pirates, whether in the Mediterranean, the South China Sea or the Strait of Malacca, threatened the flow of free trade, they were seen as threats to global economic development in general and to the interests of the British, Dutch, Americans and other Western powers in particular.

Not only did the inducement to police the oceans increase as international maritime trade surged, but also the capacity of the Western navies to do so increased after the end of the Napoleonic Wars in 1815. The political and financial consolidation of the European states, particularly Great Britain, provided the governments of those countries with unprecedented resources to equip and maintain regular naval forces that increasingly came to be stationed at naval bases around the world. The expansion of regular European naval power, and the advancement in ship building and military technology, also meant that privateering no longer was either necessary or efficient as an instrument of maritime warfare, and in 1856 most major European powers (but not the United States) signed a treaty waiving the right to use privateers in times of war.

In Southeast Asia, these developments coincided with the largest and most serious wave of piratical activity ever in the region. In the Strait of Malacca and surrounding waters, piracy by the *orang laut* and other groups in the area surged from the end of the eighteenth century, largely as a consequence of the decline of the indigenous states in the region.[10] From about the same time, large raiding fleets – sometimes composed of hundreds of vessels carrying thousands of men – set out each year from the Sulu archipelago in the southern Philippines, swarming through Southeast Asian waters from the Strait of Malacca in the west to the Moluccas in the east. The pirate fleets set out with the southwest monsoon, which usually started in the Philippines in early May, and three months later they reached the Malay peninsula, where the months from August to October became known as the 'pirate season' and the monsoon itself was referred to as the 'pirate wind'.[11]

The Sulu raiders mainly came from several nominally Muslim ethnic groups – or 'pirate tribes' (*Piratenstämme*) in the characterisation of a nineteenth-century German ethnographer[12] – based in the southern parts of the Philippines, an area over which the Spanish in the northern parts of the Philippines never had gained more than piecemeal control. The most important of these tribes were the Illanun (or Iranun), from where the Malay word for 'pirate', *lanun*, is derived, and the Samal, a group of sea nomads. Most of the large-scale raids, however, were sponsored by influential aristocrats belonging to a third ethnic group in the area, the Tausug – literally the 'people of the current' – whose homeland was the island of Jolo in the heart of the Sulu archipelago.[13]

With the advantage of swift boats powered by sail and oars, the Sulu pirates attacked both coastal settlements and vessels in annual raids throughout maritime Southeast Asia. At sea, the main targets were Asian trading vessels – Chinese as well as local – which the pirates generally preferred to the larger and more heavily armed European vessels. The loot taken by the pirates included money, valuables and weapons but also whole ships, cargoes and equipment. The main objective of the raiders, however, was to procure slaves, and from the end of the eighteenth century until the mid-nineteenth century thousands of seafarers and coastal dwellers, including not only indigenous people but also a number of Chinese, Americans and Europeans, were enslaved by the raiders and brought back to their homeland in the Sulu archipelago.

Some of the slaves were employed for household work and for manning the oars of the pirate fleets, but most were used to collect natural products, such as sea cucumber (*tripang*), bird's nests, wax, camphor, mother of pearl and tortoise shell, all of which were exported in large quantities to China. The region's integration in the China trade brought about the rapid political and economic ascendancy of the Sulu Sultanate from the last decades of the eighteenth century, and a vibrant international market – which included slaves and plunder from pirate raids – developed on Jolo. In return for the sea cucumbers and other natural products exported to China, guns, gunpowder, opium, textiles and other manufactured goods were imported to the Sulu region.[14] The imported goods served to strengthen the power and prestige of the Tausug chiefs and allowed them to launch ever larger and better-equipped raiding expeditions.

Although the overall pattern of Sulu trade and raiding in the late eighteenth and early nineteenth centuries is reasonably clear, the reasons for the surge in piratical activity and slave raiding are still insufficiently understood. European observers at the time tended to see Sulu piracy – as well as other piratical activity in the region – as a symptom of the decline, or marginalisation, of indigenous communities caused by the penetration of European and Chinese trade and other economic activity in the region.[15] More recently, among others, James Warren has questioned this so-called 'decay' theory, emphasising instead the successful integration of the Tausug chiefs and their pirate clients in the global economy. The surge in piracy and slave raiding, from this perspective, was not a symptom of decline but rather constituted a successful adaptation, or even manipulation, of global capitalism by the Tausug aristocrats.[16]

The truth probably lies somewhere in the middle ground. The Tausug aristocrats and their Illanun and Samal clients were undoubtedly successful for a sustained period of time, and the Jolo Sultanate prospered economically and politically as a result of the raiding and trade in natural products procured by the slaves. Until the mid-nineteenth century, the British, Dutch and Spanish in Southeast Asia fought an uphill battle against the Sulu pirates, clearly lacking the capacity to impose law and order on the sea and the coast. The raiders enjoyed a decisive tactical advantage as their boats generally outran the European naval vessels – even the fast frigates, the main purpose of which was to fight pirates and privateers – and, in addition, drew less water.

The situation changed dramatically, however, with the arrival of steam navigation and improvements in military technology, particularly the development of more powerful naval guns, in the course of the nineteenth century. From the 1840s and over the following decades European and American steam-powered gunboats defeated the raiding fleets of the Sulu pirates and destroyed their sanctuaries in the Sulu archipelago and elsewhere in the region. The eradication of piracy went hand in hand with the colonial expansion – in part because of a genuine commitment by the Western powers to clear the oceans of the *hostis humani generis* and in part because the prevalence of piracy provided a convenient justification, or even pretext, for territorial expansion. As James Brooke, the 'White Raja' of Sarawak in northern Borneo, and other proponents of European colonialism in the field realised, it was easier to convince public opinion at home – including those significant, mainly liberal, politicians and members of the public who opposed colonial expansion as a principle – of the need to suppress piracy and safeguard the oceans for British trade rather than of the justice in conquering and subjugating indigenous rulers and tribes.[17]

The annual 'pirate wind' thus ceased from the mid-nineteenth century, but piracy and raiding in and around the Sulu region continued throughout the nineteenth century. Even though the Spanish gradually expanded their influence in the southern Philippines, they never managed to gain effective control over the region. The northeastern part of Borneo, meanwhile, came under the control of the financially and administratively weak British North Borneo Company which also was unable to prevent piratical activity. As a result, piracy and raiding continued, as testified by William Pryer, a British official who visited Sandakan Bay on the east coast of North Borneo some 30 years after the destruction of the main pirate nests in Sulu:

> When I arrived here in 1878 I found the only place in this bay to be a small village hidden away in an obscure corner at the far end. The entrance was frequently blocked by pirates and the reason given to me for the small trade with surrounding islands was the danger of the navigation caused by them. [...] The coast line was in the hands of the rapacious Sooloos [Sulus] by whom the natives of the foreshore (Bajaus) were ground down and oppressed in every way; the natives of the forest (Booloodoopies) were forced to yield to their exactions to such an extent that but very few years more would have witnessed the extermination of large sections of them. The natives of the interior, of whom virtually nothing was known, did their best to keep themselves as far from the Sooloo crease as possible.[18]

It was not until after Spain ceded the Philippines to the United States in 1898 that Sulu piracy was effectively suppressed. After a surge in piratical activity in the first decade of the twentieth century, the Americans introduced anti-piracy patrols in the region, and in a series of bloody so-called 'pacification' campaigns between 1903 and 1913, they brought most of the southern Philippines under central government control. The region was never fully integrated with the rest of the Philippines, but law and order at sea seem to have been relatively well maintained until the outbreak of World War II in the area in 1941.[19]

In suppressing Southeast Asian piracy, the Europeans and Americans were convinced that they had restored the peaceful conditions and 'normalised' the situation after the great surge in piratical activity from the late eighteenth to the mid-nineteenth centuries. However, as the French historian Denys Lombard has remarked, they may only have substituted one form of exploitation for another.[20] In the process, all of maritime Southeast Asia had come under colonial control, and the free trade which the colonial regimes so vigorously defended was more favourable to the mother countries in Europe and North America than to most of the indigenous population of the region. Moreover, from a Southeast Asian perspective, the European, and essentially liberal, notion of *mare liberum*, or freedom on the high seas, had no historical precedent.[21] Just as in the West, political power rested, in the last instance, on coercion, but in maritime Southeast Asia this coercion was generally not territorially restricted in the fixed sense of the European nation-states. In areas such as the Strait of Malacca and the Sulu archipelago, political power traditionally relied on the domination of strategic waterways, and the use of violence through the deployment of piratical forces was a key element in the process of state formation. In that context, the new, externally imposed regime of global economic integration, free trade and fixed boundaries – on land as well as at sea – meant that the power of the region's traditional rulers and dominating groups was emasculated and substituted for new – but not necessarily less exploitative – systems of political and economic domination.

The new post-colonial states that emerged in Southeast Asia after 1945 inherited the idea of a system of sovereign states with fixed maritime and territorial boundaries. In principle, the maritime authorities – navy, marine police or coastguard – of each state were to be responsible for maintaining law and order on sea within the narrow three-mile territorial water limit, whereas the responsibility outside this limit was less clear. The international political and economic system that thus emerged in Southeast Asia after 1945 contained several actors – governments in the region and outside as well as commercial agents – whose aims and priorities in the maritime sphere differed substantially. Under these circumstances, piracy, as we shall see, could again flourish after its brief but effectual suppression during the late colonial period.

Notes

1 Pennell (1994) has identified four examples of regions that are geographically adapted to piracy: the eastern Mediterranean, the western Mediterranean, the Strait of Malacca and the south China coast. Another two can easily be identified: the Caribbean and the Sulu region comprising the present-day southern Philippines, eastern Malaysia and the Celebes Sea.

2 Fa-hsien (1956: 77).

3 Cribb (2000: 76); see also Andaya and Andaya (2001: 26) and Hall (1985).

4 See Wolters (1967: 187).

5 Cited by Wheatley (1961: 82).

6 For Melaka's role in the region during the 'Age of Commerce', see Reid (1993).

7 Cribb (2000: 105). For the Portuguese maritime empire in Asia, see Boxer (1985).

8 Rodger (2004: 115).

9 Pérotin-Dumon (2001: 33).

10 See Tarling (1978) and Trocki (1979).

11 Warren (2002: 261); see also Rutter (1986).

12 Blumentritt (1882: 51).

13 For the ethnic origins of the Sulu raiders, see Warren (2002: 25–52 and *passim*). The following summary of Sulu raiding in the late eighteenth and early nineteenth centuries is based on Warren's account.

14 Warren (1981: xv).

15 See Tarling (1978).

16 See Warren (2002).

17 For James Brooke's characterisation of the Iban of Sarawak as pirates, see Pringle (1970: 66–96).

18 Cited in Tregonning (1965: 186–187).

19 Hurley (1997: chs 23 and 25). See also Russel (1981) for the American pacification campaigns. Piracy, however, seems to have continued sporadically in the first decades of the twentieth century; see the discussion in Chapter 4, also Tagliacozzo (2000: 75).

20 Lombard (1979: 249).

21 The doctrine was first formulated in 1609 by the Dutch jurist Hugo Grotius, expressing the interests of the most formidable trading state of the age, the (Dutch) United Provinces; see Knutsen (1997: 100). In 1918 the United States President Woodrow Wilson included the doctrine as the second of his 14 points, prescribing the 'absolute freedom of navigation upon the seas', and after World War II, it was incorporated into the 1958 United Nations Convention on the Law of the Sea (UNCLOS), later superseded by the 1982 UNCLOS. For the development of the international Law of the Sea, see Sanger (1987).

Map 2: Gulf of Thailand

CHAPTER 3

Terror in the Gulf of Thailand

THE EXODUS OF INDOCHINESE BOAT REFUGEES across the Gulf of Thailand followed the Communist victories in 1975 in South Vietnam, Laos and Cambodia. For various reasons – including fear of persecution, a longing for freedom, economic motives, the wish to avoid military service or to join their families overseas – close to one and half million people fled their home countries to non-Communist countries in East and Southeast Asia. The main countries of first asylum were Thailand, Malaysia, Hong Kong and Indonesia, each of which received hundreds of thousands of refugees in the period from 1975 to 1995. The exodus reached its peak between 1977 and 1979, but large numbers of people continued to leave Indochina each year throughout the 1980s and early 1990s.[1]

Although most of the refugees arriving in Thailand were Laotians and Cambodians who travelled overland to Thailand., well over a hundred thousand Vietnamese, mostly from the southern parts of the country, tried to reach the Thai mainland by crossing the Gulf of Thailand, often in small, unseaworthy and overcrowded vessels. Many of the boat refugees were comparatively well-off professionals and businessmen who took their life-time savings and possessions with them in easily portable and exchangeable forms such as cash, gold and jewellery. Few of the vessels were armed, in part because of fears of punishment for illegally carrying arms and in part because of fears of escalating the violence in case they were attacked. The exodus of Vietnamese boat refugees thus produced a steady flow of richly loaded and defenceless vessels, providing pirates with an unprecedented opportunity to attack, loot and abuse the hapless refugees.

The pirate attacks were of two main types in terms of the levels of violence used. The first – which appears to have started somewhat earlier in the second half of the 1970s – was the less violent, opportunistic type of piracy that mainly seems to have been perpetrated by Thai fishermen-turned-pirates. The second type was the more violent and brutal type, appearing to have involved not only fishermen but also professional, organised criminals.

In 1978 Truong Nhu Tang, a former Vietnamese minister of justice, experienced an opportunistic pirate attack as his refugee boat was boarded by a large trawler in the Gulf of Thailand:

> As I watched, twenty or so young Thais clambered onto our boat, grasping a variety of weapons, long knives, hatchets, hammers, but no guns. Looking at their faces, which appeared simple rather than vicious, it registered on me that these were fishermen-pirates rather than the professional cutthroats who terrorized the Boat People. Everyone knew that many poor Thai fishermen supplemented their meagre livings by robbing refugees who happened near their boats. Encounters with thieves of this sort always left the refugees poorer, but seldom resulted in the butchery and rapine that were the trademarks of the professionals. Our pirates rounded everybody up on deck and threatened us. Then they searched us and the boat, taking our money, jewellery, and a few shirts that caught their fancy. They also liberated our compass and binoculars. But they left us food and water, and they pointed us toward the sea lanes before climbing back on their trawler and sailing off. Afterward we called them our honorable pirates.[2]

The opportunistic attacks seem to have been the work of a relatively small minority of Thai fishermen. Many fishermen did not rob the refugees whom they came upon but only lent them their assistance, giving them supplies, helping them to repair their engines and vessels and towing them to safety on the mainland. In 1982 Jack Bailey, a former United States colonel who headed a voluntary rescue operation for the boat refugees, estimated that only some 300

Thai fishing boats – two per cent of the Thai fishing fleet – were engaged in piracy.[3]

From the second half of 1979, however, numerous stories of the second, more brutal type of attacks began to attract the attention of both international media and the United Nations High Commissioner for Refugees (UNHCR).[4] The experiences related by most victims conformed to a similar overall pattern. On approaching the Thai mainland, after several days of sailing or drifting, the refugee boats were attacked by one or several Thai vessels, generally fishing boats, carrying between 10 and 20 men armed with firearms as well as simpler weapons such as knives, hammers and hatchets. The first band of pirates robbed the refugees of most of their gold and other valuables. Often, they also rammed the refugee boats and wrecked the engine or part of the hull. In several instances, the men and the women were separated and the women, frequently 11–12-year-old girls as well, were taken aboard the pirate ship to be raped, often by several men. In most instances, the hostages were then allowed to return to their damaged or sinking vessels, but the more attractive girls and women were frequently abducted by the pirates. Those refugees who attempted to resist the pirates, or who were too exhausted to comply with their wishes, were shot, beaten or thrown overboard. After the attack – unless their boat sank – the refugees then drifted until attacked by one or several other bands of pirates who carried out similar atrocities as the first group. The subsequent perpetrators often also searched the refugee boat more carefully than the first band of pirates, stealing not only whatever valuables were left after the first attack but also supplies, equipment, clothes and other personal belongings.

The following account, recorded from witness reports by the Boat People S.O.S., a United States-based non-government organisation, describes in horrific detail the fate of a group of 42 refugees who left Vietnam for the Thai mainland on 20 March 1980 in a 13-metre-long junk. Before crossing the Gulf of Thailand, the junk was intercepted by a Vietnamese navy vessel, the crew of which robbed the refugees of their valuables. Two days later, they encountered the first band of Thai pirates:

> At 3 p.m. on Mar. 22, a Thai pirate boat attacked them, searching the refugees, wrecking the motor and then letting them go. The junk drifted on and the next morning the scene was repeated. The third time came that afternoon when 2 pirate boats came upon them at once. Both vessels had cloths spread over their bows to hide their numbers. At the time, 3 Vietnamese youths were standing on the bow of the junk holding out a sail. All of a sudden the pirates fired into the three. Nguyen Van Y., 29, was struck by a bullet and fell while his brother-in-law, Nguyen Ngoc Ly, 32, a former air force officer, ran to break the fall. The pirates shot him, too. Then the pirates leaped onto the junk and threw the victims into the sea. Ly and Y., only wounded by the gunshots, struggled to get back to the boat, but they were beaten off by the pirates. [...]
>
> The remaining 40 refugees were driven onto the pirate vessel. The men were put in the ice hold and the women were raped. After that, they forced everyone back on the junk and left. The refugees continued to drift without an engine to power them. They had run out of food and water.
>
> On Mar. 24, they met another pirate boat. In terror the women smeared their faces and bodies with viscous oil, hoping in this way to repulse the pirates, but this plan did not deter the attackers who went on with the raping. They pounded holes in the junk, pried up boards as they searched for hidden gold and finally took with them two girls, Nguyen Thi A., 16, and Le Thi Y., 18.[5]

Statistics from the UNHCR show that such incidents were not isolated events befalling a minority of the refugees. In 1981 – the first year for which the High Commissioner kept such statistics – 349 boats, or 77 per cent of all recorded arriving boats, were attacked before reaching the Thai mainland.[6] As for the last months of 1979 and 1980, there are no figures available but there are reasons to believe that the problem was at least as widespread in that period as it was in 1981. The number of refugees reaching Thailand in 1980 was about the same as in 1981, and there are plenty of credible accounts by pirate victims in 1979 and 1980. During most of 1981, moreover, the Royal Thai Navy, with bilateral assistance from the United States, conducted anti-piracy missions which probably had some deterring effect on the pirates compared with the previous year.[7]

The 1981 statistics show that most of the boats were attacked more than once with an average of 3.3 times per boat, giving a total of 1,122 recorded attacks in 1981. Out of the refugees on these boats, 454 people were killed by pirates, 571 women were raped and 228 people, mostly girls and young women, were abducted.[8] These gruesome figures are probably underestimations because they only record those attacks to which there were surviving witnesses among the victims. In addition, the number of rape victims is probably also underestimated because feelings of guilt, shame and embarrassment discouraged many victims from reporting such abuses.

After having been attacked repeatedly at sea, many of the refugees who arrived in southern Thailand between 1979 and 1982 were eventually taken by pirate bands to Koh Kra, an uninhabited jungle island 130 kilometres southeast of Koh Samui. The island – which today is marketed as a haven for divers and snorkelers – was, in the words of Pascal Boulanger, transformed by the pirates into an 'immense and repugnant brothel'.[9] Shortly after the junk described in the testimony above had been robbed for the fifth time, another pirate boat attacked and towed the refugees to Koh Kra:

> [Seven] other pirate vessels were there waiting when they arrived. What ensued could only be described as chaos. The different bands fought over the valuables and women. The 11 women left, with ages ranging from 12–43, were the victims of the most vicious rape right on the beach when everyone was exhausted, hungry, thirsty and sick and their bodies still slimy with oil.
>
> Ms. Vo Thi No., 40, with her 2 daughters, aged 14 and 12, were all three raped at the same time. The pirates didn't bother to take them off to some hidden place, but went right ahead with their rape there on the beach in front of everyone.

> The next days, from Mar. 24 to April 1, hundreds of pirates from numerous boat [sic] poured onto the island and barbarous scenes took place each day: the hunting of women and the torture of men. The women spread out, some hiding in the jungle, some climbing the mountain, but by now the pirates were well acquainted with the territory and kept up the search. Sometimes they set fire to the jungle to drive the women out.[10]

The Vietnamese author Nhat Tien was part of another group of 81 refugees who were taken to Koh Kra in October 1979. The island was deserted when they arrived but on the second day a Thai navy vessel visited the island. The uniformed crew collected information from the refugees and promised that they would return later. They never did, however, and on the following day, the terror began for the refugees:

> As dusk fell, a band of Thai fishermen bearing rifles, hammers and knives came to us with torches. They gave us a thorough search, took some clothing and then went away. Just after they were gone, another band came to take their place, searching us everywhere and this continued until beyond midnight. All in all there were three bands that did this. The last one, completing their search, drove all the men and youths into a cave and stood guard over it while they took the women away to rape them. In the dark mist and the cold wind, we could only listen to the cries of the children being torn from their mothers' arms, the prayers and beseeching of the feeble women. [...] Women were pulled out of some spots and beaten, and then gang raped cruelly by as many as ten fishermen at a time. Some pirates engaged in sadistic sex, striking the victims as they raped them until the girls fainted. One person was beaten continuously in the abdomen so much that it even now is painful.[11]

The boys and men were also terrorised by the pirates:

> Some of us were beaten and forced to point out their hiding places, others were choked with a chord to make them

> divulge where gold or dollars were supposedly hidden. Most tragic was a case where a man tried to save the virtue of a relation of his. First he was hit with an ax [sic] till his forehead split open then he was thrown on the rocky shore. By some luck he did not die then and there. One old gentleman with a few gold teeth had these pried out with a knife.[12]

During the 15 days that Nhat Tien spent on Koh Kra, hundreds of pirates came to harass the refugees, and several new groups of refugees were brought to the island by different bands of pirates. Sometimes, there were up to 40–50 boats jamming the entrance to the island.[13]

Few of the refugees had any valuables left, and rape therefore was apparently the main objective of the pirates who came to Koh Kra. Although the perpetrators, from the accounts of witnesses, seem to have been driven by debauchery, there may also have been more organised motives behind the raping. According to European humanitarian organisations working in Thailand in the mid-1980s, large numbers of prostitutes in brothels in Bangkok were Vietnamese boat refugees who had come through Koh Kra.[14] In this context, the mass rapings on the island may have been part of a deliberate strategy to install feelings of shame and guilt in the victims, thus preparing them for commercial sexual exploitation. According to UNHCR figures, a total of 694 boat refugees, almost exclusively women, were abducted between 1981 and 1987, 381 of whom were never unaccounted for.[15]

The trafficking of female refugees for sexual purposes indicates that organised criminal gangs may have been involved the attacks. The extent and brutality of the rapes, moreover, also suggest the involvement of hardened professional criminals. One account of a pirate attack on 30 January 1980, for example, relates how seven women – six of whom subsequently were abducted – were attacked and raped by 70 pirates from 13 different boats:

> The pirates did not rape in any orderly manner, but pulled all the women out on the floor, turned on the lights and

> gathered around, laughing and joking raucously as they waited their turns. Bui Doan reports his clear recollection that the band of pirates from the boat #1544 were the most vicious. Their faces were painted, leaving only the white eyes exposed and their stripped bodies were tatooed in strange designs; one man's face was tatooed as well. These men wore various kinds of unusual medals. One even wore his pistol at his side.[16]

This image of the Thai pirates seems to confirm that the pirates were members of organised criminal gangs. According to the witnesses, moreover, the boat which had initiated the attack was not a normal fishing boat, but made of iron and equipped with radar.[17] This description conforms to the testimony of Jack Bailey before the United States Congress about the character and organisation of the pirates. According to Baily, the professional pirates operated in international waters, 20–30 miles (32–48 kilometres) off the coast with large boats equipped with good radar and radios.[18] Often, they were also armed with automatic weapons. In his testimony, Bailey also revealed that many Thai fishermen suffered at the hands of pirates and he claimed that an average of five Thai fishing trawlers per month were lost due to pirate attacks in 1982. He also said that over the previous two years, 500 Thai fishermen had been killed by pirates. The activities and *modus operandi* of the pirates were well known by local authorities, but because of corruption, the pirates enjoyed protection.[19]

The organised pirates in the Gulf of Thailand not only attacked boat refugees and fishermen, but also merchant vessels and yachts passing through the area. According to Thai government sources, reported by the International Maritime Bureau in 1985, one pirate gang used specially designed speedboats to attack passenger and merchant vessels in the area.[20] Roger Villar, moreover, has recounted an incident in which a yachter, who was attacked by pirates armed with carbines off Nakorn Si Thammarat in southern Thailand in 1979, killed two of the attackers and wounded one. The wounded pirate was rescued and later admitted that the group was part of a protection racket, controlled by a rich local landowner, that specialised in extorting money from fishing boats in the area.[21]

Those refugees who did not perish on Koh Kra or were trafficked to prostitution were eventually – often after several weeks of continuous terror – rescued from the island and taken to the Thai mainland. Most of the rescue operations were led by the UNCHR's field officer, Theodore Schweitzer, sometimes with the assistance of the Thai police. Schweitzer first arrived in Koh Kra in mid-1979, and he then found evidence everywhere of earlier attacks against the refugees, including warning messages written in Vietnamese on navigational structures, letters warning of rape and abductions and dead bodies.[22] Between the last months of 1979 and the first months of 1982, Schweitzer made at least two dozen return trips to Koh Kra saving 1,250 refugees.[23] In 1983, he founded the private humanitarian organisation Southeast Asia Rescue Foundation to assist the Indochinese refugees. This initiative, together with other initiatives by private individuals and voluntary organisations, provided much needed help for the boat refugees throughout the 1980s.[24]

After their rescue to the Thai mainland, several of the pirates' victims reported the abuses to the Thai police. In November 1979, the testimonies of the group of refugees to which Nhat Tien belonged led to the arrest of a group of seven pirates in Pakpanang in southern Thailand. In the nearby district capital of Nakhon Si Thammarat, moreover, another group of seven alleged pirates were arrested for taking part in gang rapes on Koh Kra. The latter group was recognised by their victims as they crewed a small trawler hired by the police to evacuate the refugees from Koh Kra.[25]

According to Nhat Tien, the arrest of the Pakpanang group was made after the pirates happened to be sighted and recognised when they passed by the place where the refugees were staying. Both during the police investigation and the subsequent trial, the refugees, who according to Thai law were not allowed to be plaintiffs but were instead called as witnesses, were subject of threats, harassment and attempts of bribery, both by officials and by relatives of the accused pirates, to force them to withdraw their testimonies. According to

Nhat Tien, none of the defendants ever appeared at the trial which dragged on from January to June 1980. The witnesses, by contrast, were called one by one and forced to stand up during the whole eight-hour sessions of the court. The witnesses, particularly the rape victims, were also reportedly subject to a range of irrelevant and intimidating questions by the court.[26]

If – as, indeed, it seems – it was the deliberate strategy of the court to delay and obstruct the conviction of the pirates, this was not entirely successful. The trials attracted considerable attention in national Thai media, and from the end of June, a Thai lawyer representing the United Nations observed the proceedings in Pakpanang, which apparently helped to expedite the proceedings.[27] In June 1980, the seven pirates who had been arrested in Pakpanang were sentenced to heavy prison terms, varying from 8 to 24 years, for gang robbery, false imprisonment and rape.[28]

The heavy punishments, however, were an exception. Five other trials were held in the same year, with charges of robbery, theft, abduction, rape and murder being brought against a total of 20 alleged perpetrators. The result of these trials was that 15 of the defendants were acquitted and five were sentenced to short prison terms of six months for minor offences.[29] Meanwhile, the pirates continued to roam the Gulf of Thailand and new groups of refugees were taken to Koh Kra to be terrorised.

Against this background of impunity for the pirates and what appeared to be passivity on the part of Thai authorities to stem the problem, some observers, including the United Nations High Commissioner for Refugees Poul Hartling, seemed convinced that the government tacitly permitted, or even encouraged, piracy as part of a deliberate strategy to deter the refugees from coming to Thailand.[30] One analyst even argued that public opinion in Thailand saw the flow of refugees as part of mass invasion plan and that, in this context, the pirates might 'form a first line of defence for the Thais against Vietnam'.[31] Coincidentally or not, the violent and organised attacks apparently increased sharply in the second half of 1979, shortly after Indonesia, Malaysia, the Philippines, Singapore and

Thailand, which together comprised the then five members of the Association of Southeast Asian Nations (ASEAN), issued a statement rejecting further arrivals of Indochinese refugees.[32]

If indeed the pirate attacks were part of a deliberate strategy of deterrence, the policy looks to have worked well. Between 1981 and 1982, boat refugee arrivals in Thailand dropped by 62 per cent, from over 15,000 to less than 6,000, and the number of arrivals continued to decline in the following years.[33] Even though the decline in part may be attributable to other factors – notably Thailand's policy of so-called 'humane deterrence' which included the downgrading of conditions in refugee camps and not allowing refugees who reached Thailand from Vietnam to resettle in a third country – it seems likely that the frequency and brutality of the pirate attacks against the refugees in 1979 and subsequent years had a considerable deterring effect. Through international media and correspondence with friends and relatives abroad, most refugees leaving Vietnam, at least from 1981 onward, were probably well aware of the fate that in preceding years had befallen their compatriots at the hand of the Thai pirates.[34]

Nor did the refugees get much help from commercial vessels passing through the area, in spite of an appeal by the High Commissioner for Refugees Poul Hartling for shipmasters to uphold maritime traditions and international law by assisting refugee boats in distress. According to the International Maritime Bureau, many of the Vietnamese refugee boats that arrived in Thailand and other coastal states in Southeast Asia with dead or dying refugees on board reported being passed by commercial vessels ignoring their distress signals.[35]

Responding to international criticism, Thai officials claimed that they did not have enough fast patrol boats to police effectively the country's long coastline and territorial waters.[36] Gradually, the international community also began to realise that financial assistance to the Thai government might be necessary to combat piracy in the area. Already in May 1980, the UNHCR donated an unarmed speedboat to the Thai government in a token effort to boost its maritime policing capacity. A few months later, the Royal Thai Navy boarded two suspected pirate vessels in what was the first known case of such a boarding. Early the following year, the United States government initiated a US$ 2 million bilateral anti-piracy programme under which the Thai navy employed two spotter aircraft and a coastguard cutter to combat the pirates. Although these measures probably had some deterring effect on the pirates and resulted in the seizure of five vessels and the arrest of 25 alleged pirates, it was insufficient to root out the problem. The programme was also criticised for its over-commitment to expensive air surveillance, and within eight months, it had run out of money.[37]

In June 1982, after some delay, a more comprehensive US$ 3.6 million programme was launched, funded by 12 countries and channelled through the UNHCR. The programme – which involved 130 personnel from the Royal Thai Navy, Marine Police and Harbour Departments – included both air and sea surveillance, as well as land-based intelligence operations and a fishing boat registration project designed to facilitate the identification of possible culprits. An anti-piracy post was stationed on Koh Kra in order to prevent the pirates from using the island as a base.[38]

The anti-piracy efforts managed to bring about a substantial decline in pirate attacks from its peak in 1981. To some extent, the sharp drop in the absolute number of attacks – down by 67 per cent from 1,122 in 1981 to 373 in 1982 – was probably due to the decline in the flow of refugees. The percentage of boats attacked also declined, however, from 77 to 64 per cent, and the average number of pirate attacks per arriving boat decreased from 2.5 in 1981 to 1.7 in 1982. The decline in pirate attacks continued in the following years, so that in 1986, the UNHCR only recorded 87 attacks against 13 per cent of the boats and the average number of attacks per arriving boat was down to 1.5.[39]

These numbers, however, conceal considerable regional variation. Those parts of the Gulf of Thailand that were particularly pirate-infested included the waters to the north and south of the Isthmus of Kra, where pirates reportedly operated out of Pakphanang, Srichon and Chumphon, and the waters off the Trat and Chanthaburi provinces southeast of Bangkok, near the Cambodian border.[40] Even though the UNHCR-sponsored anti-piracy operations were headed from Songkhla in southern Thailand, the decline in piracy was most marked in the waters southeast of Bangkok, where the percentage of boats attacked declined drastically from around 65 per cent in the early 1980s to between 4 and 5 per cent in 1986–1987. The corresponding figure for southern Thailand, by contrast, was 44 per cent in 1986.[41] A substantial number of the boats arriving in Malaysia were also attacked, even though the percentage declined by half from 27 per cent in 1985 to 13 per cent in 1987.[42]

The levels of violence showed a corresponding decline between 1981 and 1987. In the 1987, there were no reports of deaths due to piracy, and the number of rapes and abductions also substantially decreased.[43] In the following year, however, piratical violence returned with a vengeance, as more than 500 people were reported dead or missing.[44] The figure increased further in 1989, when the number of people killed exceeded 750 and the UNHCR estimated that up to 20 per cent of the refugees fleeing Vietnam were killed at the hands of pirates.[45] Courtland Robinson, who has done extensive re-search on the exodus of Vietnamese refugees between 1975 and 1995, has suggested two possible reasons for the surge in violence towards the end of the 1980s. First, the anti-piracy efforts had eliminated the more opportunistic – and presumably less violence-prone – pirates, leaving behind a hard core of more violently inclined professional criminals. Second, the pirates may have taken greater pains not to leave any witnesses – a suspicion which seems to be confirmed by the accounts of those occasional witnesses who did survive.[46]

In the second half of the 1980s, the number of Vietnamese refugees to Thailand began to decrease and in the first years of the 1990s, the flow was reduced to a trickle. Pirate attacks also subsided, and in 1991 the UNHCR anti-piracy programme was discontinued. Although piracy in the Gulf of Thailand had not been completely stamped out, it could, according to the final assessment report of the High Commissioner, be effectively managed by local agencies.[47]

Attempts to explain the surge in piracy against the Vietnamese boat refugees in the Gulf of Thailand have so far generally focused on either economic or political factors. The economic explanation – generally favoured by Thai official sources – typically highlights the supposedly opportunistic character of the attacks. In this version, the defenceless boat refugees are seen as naturally tempting prizes for impoverished Thai fishermen.[48] Poverty and opportunism, however, fails to explain why piracy suddenly occurred with such ferocity from the second half of 1979, and why it almost exclusively occurred in the Gulf of Thailand, and not, for example, to any great extent in Indonesian or Philippine waters. Mere opportunity also seems weak as an explanation for the brutal mass rapings and killings, both in the beginning of the 1980s and towards the end of the decade.

The political explanations, by contrast, tend to see the attacks as part of a tacit strategy of deterrence by the Thai government. As with conspiracy theories in general, however, the main problem – apart from the ethical dimension – is the lack of concrete evidence to substantiate such allegations. The reported lack of concern for the well-being of the refugees on the part of sections of the law enforcement authorities does not in itself prove that the Thai government condoned piracy in order to deter the refugees. The failure to protect the refugees was probably to a great extent due to insufficiency and inefficiency on the part of the authorities.

Even if the conspiracy theories are left out, however, political factors go a long way to explain the outbreak of piracy in the Gulf of Thailand from the end of the 1970s. In the eyes of the Vietnamese government, the refugees were traitors, or at least lacking in patriotism, and the country's navy could apparently attack the refugee boats with impunity even before they had left Vietnamese waters. The Thai government, meanwhile, was more concerned about the social and economic strain that the large flow of refugees caused, and it was not a high priority to protect these refugees, especially not in international waters where most attacks occurred. The United States and other Western countries did provide assistance, notably in the form of financial assistance, for an anti-piracy programme, but it was underfinanced, slow to come about, and was unable to prevent thousands of refugees from being robbed and killed by what seemed to be professional pirates in the last years of the 1980s. The anti-piracy programme, moreover, was administered by the UNHCR, indicating that the issue was neither seen as an international security problem nor as an international maritime issue, in which case it would have been handled by the Maritime Safety Committee of the IMO. Rather, it was regarded as a locally confined refugee problem and, as such, not very high on any government's or international political organisation's agenda.

Notes

1 United Nations High Commissioner for Refugees (2000: 98). See further Robinson (1998) for an authoritative account of the Indo-chinese exodus and the international response.

2 Truong Nhu Tang (1986: 304–305).

3 Committee on Foreign Affairs (1982: 62).

4 It is uncertain when exactly these attacks started, but they seem only to have attracted international attention from 1979. The UNHCR first reported on the problem to United Nations General Assembly in its 1979 report; see 'Report of the United Nations High Commissioner for Refugees', UN, A/35/12, Supplement no. 12, items 29 and 300. The chronology of pirate attacks in the Gulf of Thailand compiled by Roger Villar (1985: 131–139) lists the first incident in November 1979. Robinson (1998: 60) also implies that the attacks only started in the second half of 1979. The *Far Eastern Economic Review* carried its first article on the subject on 1 February 1980. None of the accounts in Nhat Tien et al. (1981), moreover, relate incidents taking place before 1979.

5 Ibid. (1981: 32–33). The story was recorded on 13 April 1980, only three weeks after it took place, in the refugee camp at Songkhla in southern Thailand by investigators of the Boat People S.O.S. Committee.

6 For the UNHCR statistics, see Ellen (ed.) (1989: 282–283).

7 See Committee on Foreign Affairs (1982: 84). For the anti-piracy efforts, see further below.

8 Ellen (ed.) (1989: 282). The number of rape victims does not include those girls and women who were abducted, most of whom also presumably were raped or otherwise sexually abused.

9 Boulanger (1989: 85).

10 Nhat Tien et al. (1981: 34).

11 Ibid. (1981: 82–84).

12 Ibid. (1981: 84).

13 The number of boats is confirmed by the UNHCR representative in the area, Theodore Schweitzer, who during one flight over the island counted 47 boats anchored in a bay with bodies floating around them; Boulanger (1989: 85).

14 See Boulanger (1989: 88). The president of the West German humanitarian organisation Cap Anamur Committee, Ruper Neudeck, based his claim on statistics of 136 women abducted in 1985. The UNHCR officer in the area at the time, Theodore Schweitzer, also confirms that there were a number of cases in which Vietnamese refugee women were sold into prostitution; e-mail message from Theodore Schweitzer to the author, 12 September 2005.

15 Ellen (ed.) (1989: 282).

16 Nhat Tien et al. (1981: 24).

17 Ibid. (1981: 23).

18 Committee on Foreign Affairs (1982: 69).

19 Ibid. (1982: 59, 70).

20 'Piracy and armed robbery against ships. A second report into the incidence of piracy and armed robbery from merchant ships. Note by the Secretariat', IMO, MSC 50/INF.2 (10 July 1984).

21 Villar (1985: 48).

22 E-mail message from Theodore Schweitzer to the author, 12 September 2005.

23 Robinson (1998: 61). Several of the victims quoted in Nhat Tien et al. (1981) also express their gratitude to Schweitzer for rescuing them.

24 See the organisation's Internet web page at http://www.searescue.org/ accessed on 12 September 2005. The site also contains photo documentation of the rescue operations on Koh Kra.

25 *Far Eastern Economic Review* (1 February 1980).

26 Nhat Tien et al. (1981: 47–50).

27 Ibid. (1981: 50).

28 Boulanger (1989: 93).

29 Ibid (1989: 93–95). Starting in 1984, however, a greater number of the perpetrators seems to have been sentenced to long prison terms; see the summary of the sentences in Ellen (ed.) (1989: 286–289).

30 This view was for example expressed by Bayard Rustin, co-chairman of the non-government organisation Citizens Commission on Indochinese Refugees, in a hearing in the U.S. House of Representatives; see Committee on Foreign Affairs (1982: 68). A statement by 157 refugees who had been rescued from Koh Kra in November 1979 also expressed the conviction that the 'fostering of piracy has its origin [...] in the Thai government's desire to discourage the Vietnamese boat refugees from coming to Thailand by permitting improper behaviour by the pirates'; see Nhat Tien et al. (1989: 51). Commenting on the pirate attacks against the boat refugees, High Commissioner Poul Hartling was quoted in the *New York Times* (4 July 1984), saying that 'some people in Thailand have a clear position that refugees should not be there and should be kept away'; cited by Robinson (1998: 169).

31 Dupont (1986), cited by Boulanger (1989: 87).

32 United Nations High Commissioner for Refugees (2000: 83).

33 Ellen (ed.) (1989: 282).

34 The director of the United States State Department's Bureau of Refugee Programmes, Richard Vine, was convinced that the decline in refugees reaching Thailand primarily was due to the humane deterrence policy. However, he also believed that there was a high degree of awareness among the refugees leaving Vietnam about the brutality and frequency of pirate attacks in the Gulf of Thailand, and he implied that an effective anti-piracy programme might constitute a significant pull factor for the refugees to flee to Thailand; see Committee on Foreign Affairs (1982: 5, 13–14, 71).

35 ICC – International Maritime Bureau (1985: 39).

36 *Far Eastern Economic Review* (1 February 1980).

37 Robinson (1998: 167) and Boulanger (1989: 92).

38 Henkel (1989: 108) and Kasemsri (1989: 115).

39 Ellen (ed.) (1989: 282).

40 *Far Eastern Economic Review* (1 February 1980).

41 Blaney III (1989: 102).

42 Ellen (ed.) (1989: 283).

43 Ibid. (1989: 282). In 1987, there were only four abductions and 67 reported cases of rape.

44 Robinson (1998: 170).

45 Ibid. and *Daily Telegraph* (10 April 1989).

46 Robinson (1998: 171).

47 United Nations High Commissioner for Refugees (2000: 87).

48 See, e.g. Kasemsri (1989: 116) and officials of the Thai Fisheries Department, quoted in the *Far Eastern Economic Review* (1 February 1980). Theodore Schweitzer of the UNHCR also believes that the attacks were perpetrated by opportunistic fishermen rather than of organised criminals; e-mail message from Theodore Schweitzer to the author, 12 September 2005. The evidence of the involvement of organised crime is admittedly circumstantial and seems to require a more thorough historical investigation.

Map 3: Southern Philippines and eastern Malaysia

CHAPTER 4

Opportunistic Piracy

IN THE GULF OF THAILAND, as elsewhere, it is useful to distinguish between organised and non-organised (or opportunistic) piracy, with the latter type being by far the most common in Southeast Asia today and over the past decades. Opportunistic piracy is mostly perpetrated by quite small groups, generally working independently in a restricted, relatively small, local area. The attacks require little detailed information or planning ahead and involve little sophisticated equipment apart from a motor-powered vessel from which to launch the attack and some, often rudimentary, form of weapon. The motive is mostly short-term economic – or, as we shall see, social – and the profit is generally divided by the perpetrators immediately after a successful attack and used for consumption rather than reinvested in criminal or other illicit activities.

Opportunistic piracy in contemporary Southeast Asia, as well as throughout most of the post-1945 period, is concentrated in a few parts of the region, each of which broadly corresponds to a different type of attack in terms of the methods, equipment and levels of violence used. Apart from the attacks against the Vietnamese boat refugees in the Gulf of Thailand, three different types of *modus operandi* can readily be identified and linked to distinct parts of the region. The first is high-level armed robberies including coastal raids which mainly occur in the Sulu archipelago in the southern Philippines and off the east coast of Malaysian Borneo. The second type is low-level armed robberies, which mainly occur in the southern parts of the Malacca Strait (south of the 3rd parallel North), the Singapore Strait, Indonesia's Riau-Lingga archipelago and around the Bangka and Belitung islands off the Indonesian province of South Sumatra.[1] Finally, the third type is high-level armed robberies and kidnappings-for-ransom, which mainly occur in the northern parts of the Malacca Strait (north of the 3rd parallel North). In this chapter, each of the three types, their geographic distribution and historical background will be discussed at some length with the purpose of understanding the variations in piratical activity in contemporary Southeast Asia. The analysis will be mainly from a criminological perspective that takes into account what we know of the economic, social and cultural background of the perpetrators.

High-level armed robberies including coastal raids – the southern Philippines and off the east coast of Malaysian Borneo

After the American pacification campaigns of 1903–1913, piracy in the Sulu region appears to have subsided, if not ceased completely. The colonial authorities collected thousands of firearms from outlaw elements in the southern Philippines, and law and order were maintained by the Philippine Constabulary, a police force set up by the Americans, aided by naval patrol vessels.

The only piratical attack which attracted international attention during the late colonial period occurred in 1920 and involved a boat carrying eleven Dutch citizens in the Celebes Sea. The boat was attacked by a group of 24 armed 'Moros' – that is, Muslims of the southern Philippines – who abducted two of the women on board and, according to the verdict over the perpetrators in the Philippine Supreme Court in 1922, 'brutally violated [them] by methods too horrible to be described'. Before leaving the target boat the pirates made small holes in it in order that it would submerge with the remaining passengers. The boat stayed afloat, however, and the passengers were rescued after 11 days at sea. Meanwhile the abducted women were able to escape after reaching Maruro, a coastal town in the Netherlands Indies.[2]

This brutal attack seems to have been an exception to the general law and order of the late colonial period, which lasted until the Japanese attack on the American colony in December 1941. During the Japanese occupation, the security situation declined drastically and, as a direct result of the end of World War II, large numbers of modern firearms again became available in the Sulu region. The war thus signalled the end of the brief period of relatively stable conditions – at least on the surface – and pre-twentieth-century patterns of violence, including piracy and other forms of maritime violence, resumed with new vigour.[3]

The problem grew worse in the immediate post-war period as the police authorities of the newly independent Philippines were incapable of upholding law and order in the increasingly unruly southern parts of the country. In 1950, a concerned dispatch from the British Legation in Manila to London noticed that 'the Moros are reverting to type and are again finding in piracy and smuggling an easy way of making a living'.[4] A combination of protectionist policies, trade restrictions, corruption and lax law enforcement triggered a surge in activities that the central Philippine government regarded as illegal, such as the export of agricultural products, particularly copra (coconut), from the southern Philippines to British North Borneo (from 1963 the Malaysian state of Sabah) in exchange for cigarettes. Both smuggling and piracy, moreover, were facilitated by the motorisation of inter-island transport as a result of the availability of United States military surplus engines in the aftermath of the war.[5]

One of the most notorious pirates in the 1950s and 1960s was Isabelo 'Beloy' Montemayor, a master of disguises and alleged Robin Hood of the seas who, after he was killed by security forces in 1975, became the hero of, not one, but two feature films produced in the Philippines.[6] Based in Cebu in the Visayas to the northeast of the Sulu Sea, Montemayor led an organised racket that maintained a well-equipped and -manned small fleet and engaged in smuggling of cigarettes and other contraband, gun-running, maritime raiding and extortion. During night-time raids, Montemayor and his accomplices attacked and raided fish carrier boats and other inter-island vessels, including passenger vessels. Some smugglers and merchants in the coastal towns of the Visayas paid protection money to Montemayor, whereas others had their homes and stores raided by heavily armed men descending from high-speed motorised pump-boats.[7]

Apart from Montemayor's gang, most of the Philippine pirates in the post-war years seem to have come from some of the (often nominally) Muslim ethnic groups in the southern parts of the country, mainly Mindanao and the Sulu Archipelago. During the last years of British rule in North Borneo, in the late 1950s and early 1960s, both seafarers and coastal settlements in the colony suffered attacks from pirates who were believed mainly to be based in Tawi-tawi, a small group of islands in the far southwest of the Sulu Archipelago. Between 1959 and 1962, 232 pirate attacks were recorded by the British authorities, but these were thought to be no more than the tip of an iceberg as many attacks probably went unreported. There were stories of gun battles at sea as seafarers tried to fight off attackers, and some attacks probably resulted in the killing of all those on board the target ship thus leaving no witnesses to report the attack. Most of the victims were Indonesian barter traders carrying copra from North Sulawesi to ports in British North Borneo, but what concerned the British even more were several armed raids on the coastal towns and settlements of the colony, because these threatened to drive away labourers, thereby seriously affecting the local economy. In 1962 alone there were 20 armed raids on the coast of British North Borneo which left at least eight people dead and many more injured.[8] One of the most brutal raids took place at Kunak, a timber camp on the east coast:

> The raid began about 1740 hours [...] when a vessel (technically a "kumpit", but more like a Chinese launch in appearance and about 24 feet long) approached Kunak from the Semporna Channel. It had a "kajang" covering, badly maintained. At the time the government launch "Rusakan" was alongside the steps of the wharf, and the British Borneo Timber Company log towing boat, "Darvel Bay", was alongside the longest part of the wharf. As the "kumpit" came alongside the "Rusakan", the muzzles of four rifles appeared over its side. The occupants of the "kumpit" opened fire and

> in the first burst killed the Engineer of the "Rusakan", who was sitting on the forward deck, and wounded two children also on deck. The two sailors, the Engineer's wife and one of the sailor's wives jumped into the sea. The serang (skipper) was wounded in the left arm as he also jumped for the sea. The kumpit then pulled up to the wharf. Four raiders ran across the wharf to the "Darvel Bay", which had its engine running, shot four members of the crew and did some damage to the engine. One man returned to the "Rusakan", smashed the copper pipes of the engine, tore out the radio and transferred it and the "Rusakan's" binoculars to the kumpit. While one raider stayed in the kumpit, the rest, some seven in number, advanced from the wharf, with two firing up the road, while others entered the shops near the wharf and forced local people to carry goods and money back to the kumpit. The telephone-line was cut and an attempt was made to launch the Mostyn Estates launch "Lucinda". This was unsuccessful, as it was locked up. The raiders then stove in the boat and damaged the engine. [...]
>
> After the raiders had loaded their boat, they saw a Chinese launch coming in round the coral. They intercepted it, tied up their own boat to it, told the passengers to jump into the sea and ordered the skipper and engineer, named Kamaludin, to tow the kumpit out.[9]

Although information is scarce about the historical and cultural background of the Tawi-tawi pirates – the British seemed to be at a loss as to what their ethnicity was – it is possible that at least some of them were descendants of the Samal pirates who settled there after the Spanish in 1848 sacked their strongholds on the island of Balangingi east of Jolo in the heart of the Sulu Archipelago. Tawi-tawi pirates continued to conduct raids in the Philippine archipelago and along the east coast of Borneo throughout the nineteenth century, at times assembling large fleets of between 60 and 100 vessels.[10] The recent history of piracy and raiding was probably still in the collective memory of the descendants of the Samal pirates on Tawi-tawi after the end of World War II and may have contributed to making piracy culturally sanctioned, at least among some segments of the population on Tawi-tawi.[11]

Another ethnic group among whom piracy is culturally sanctioned even in modern times is the Tausug whose ethnic homeland is on Jolo, but who also have established communities on other islands of the Sulu Archipelago, including Tawi-tawi. Many reports of piratical attacks and coastal raids in the past decades allege that the perpetrators were Tausug speakers.[12] Thomas Kiefer, an American anthropologist who did fieldwork in 'Tubig Nangka', a Tausug community on the eastern part of Jolo in the 1960s, has provided the following description of piratical activity among the Tausug:

> Raids today are conducted primarily for loot rather than slaves, and they are usually only undertaken at relatively short distances: 75 miles to Basilan Island or Tawi-tawi Island, or a very occasional raid of 100 miles to Zamboanga. The traffic in smuggled cigarettes from Borneo has created new opportunities for piracy and cargoes are sometimes hijacked in an atmosphere of Byzantine intrigue. More rarely, inter-island passenger vessels are held up. Chinese merchants and wealthy Christians are a favourite target, although raids are sometimes conducted against relatively poor isolated settlements of non-Tausug Moslems; in some cases an entire village may be looted. For the most part these activities are conducted by younger men in search of fortune and adventure who in less adventurous moments are simple farmers or fishermen; fulltime "professional" pirates are rare. In Tubig Nangka, about 20 percent of the younger men had been on at least one piracy expedition outside of Jolo Island.[13]

Apart from slaves, much of the loot taken by modern Tausug pirates in the 1960s was similar to that which their great-grandfathers and earlier ascendants took in the nineteenth century: cattle, money, jewellery, weapons, brass work and gongs. In addition, new items in the 1960s included shoes, watches, transistor radios and sewing machines. Even though on a much smaller scale, the basic social organisation of pirate groups was also similar to that of the nineteenth century, consisting of more or less temporary self-defence and mutual-aid groups of between ten and 25 armed men. The group members were recruited by a leader among his kinsmen as well as friends, and a group might seek to join forces with other groups for larger expeditions.[14]

To the extent that there was a cultural sanctioning of piracy among the Tausug, however, it was not unequivocally so and was mainly confined to certain social groups, particularly young men. Among these groups, piracy was seen as a form of risk taking, which was encouraged among the men, and associated with highly regarded virtues such as bravado, honour, masculinity and magnanimity. Piratical raids to distant islands, in this context, provided an opportunity for young men to demonstrate such virtues. It was thus the elements of danger, risk and fate that provided the main motivations for Tausug piracy. According to Kiefer: 'While the desire for loot and pecuniary rewards is also important, it is the desire associated with gambling, not the pecuniary gain of everyday work, as there is always a doubt about the outcome of the mission.'[15]

A group of people that have been particularly vulnerable to the raids of the Tausug and other pirates are the Sea Gypsies (Bajau Laut) in the Sulu region. Another American anthropologist, Clifford Sather, recorded the following story from 1979 by a Bajau fisherman, who was fishing at night off the town of Semporna in eastern Sabah together with two other boat crews when they were approached by pirates:

> They called us to stop. Instead, we abandoned our nets – we had just set them out – and fled single-file across the reefs. Fortunately, the lead crew leader knew the underwater channels at night, and the pirates weren't able to follow us. As we drew out of range, we could hear them talking – debating whether to fire on us or not. We made our way to Maiga Island, where there are now lots of refugees living. We stayed there overnight. At daylight we went back to look for our nets. That was a bad time (the previous year, 1978).

> Almost every week, someone was attacked. Boats couldn't stay at sea without being robbed of their catch.[16]

In contrast to many other ethnic groups in the region, the Sea Gypsies do not have a strong tradition of violence, and only rarely carry firearms. This may in recent decades have hastened their decline in the aggressive atmosphere of the Sulu Sea where firearms – as in most of the Philippines – are widely available.[17] The proliferation of arms in the southern Philippines, moreover, has increased as a result of the armed insurgency in the region since 1972.[18] A vivid image of the armed environment in the region is Bongao, a Tausug-dominated coastal town in Tawi-tawi, which was described in the following terms by the news magazine *Asiaweek* in 1993:

> Guns are still a common sight and status symbol in Bongao: all the Tausug who spend much time on the water – fishermen and smugglers – carry pistols and rifles as a matter of course. The restaurants and pool halls are decorated with pictures of shiny, curvaceous Magnums, Berettas and Colt .45s (ironically designed for American use against the Tausug). The magazine stands stock titles like *Shooting Times* and *Gun World*. To compound our first impressions, nearly everyone we meet seems to know someone who's been attacked or killed by pirates.[19]

In the following year, the IMO's fact-finding mission on piracy and armed robbery against ships in the South China Sea observed that pirates in the Philippines had become more vicious due mainly to their being armed, mostly with low velocity weapons such as pistols, but also 'assault rifles, such as M16s, carbines, garand and AK47 rifles'.[20] Probably the problem has been exacerbated even further since the mid-1990s. In the past 12 years, Philippine authorities have reportedly recorded 431 deaths due to piratical activity in the country, along with 426 people missing.[21] The large number of missing people, most of whom presumably have drowned, is explained by the fact that many victims are ordered by the pirates to jump in the water – a practice which has caused the pirates to be known by the exhortation *ambak pare*, 'jump buddy'.[22]

The victims of the piratical activities in the region since the 1950s have mostly been sea gypsies and other local seafarers, such as small-scale traders and fishermen. According to information provided by the Philippine Coast Guard to the IMO in 1994, the main target of pirates operating in the Moro Gulf, particularly along the east coast of the Gulf off the coast of South Cotabato, was the catch of local fishing boats, especially of the valuable yellow-fin tuna. Often, however, fishermen were also robbed of boat engines, fuel, personal effects or even the entire boat.[23]

Many southern Filipino pirates seem to have little regard for human life and often seek to leave no surviving witnesses from an attack. Some reports also tell of sadism and mutilation, including victims having their ears sliced off or their knees smashed by bullets to make swimming impossible.[24] The following story, recorded by the IMB of an attack on a Philippine fishing boat in 1996, illustrates the brutality that characterises piracy in the Sulu region:

> A fishing vessel NM3-NORMINA with a crew of ten, was fishing off Basilan Island, between Sibago and Matanal Point, in the southern Philippines. At midday, suddenly two speedboats approached her, with two men in each and armed with automatic firearms. The gunmen opened fire and killed nine of the crew. The tenth, Jangay Ajinohon, was injured in the back of the head. Despite his injury, Mr. Ajinohon managed to escape by swimming away, while the pirates were busy attaching lines to the MN3-NORMINA to tow her.[25]

In terms of the levels of violence and human suffering, the Sulu region stands out as probably the most dangerous region in the world. Not only is piracy and maritime raiding culturally sanctioned among some of the maritime communities in the region; violence is also triggered by the proliferation of firearms, including modern automatic weapons, in the region since World War II. Moreover, many of the Muslim groups who traditionally inhabit the Sulu archipelago are only weakly integrated, and even marginalised, in the Philippine nation. Piratical activity, in this context, may even be seen as historically and religiously justified as a means of resistance against the attempts by Christians – whether Spanish, American or Filipinos – to control and dominate the region.

Low-level armed robberies – the southern Malacca Strait, Singapore Strait, Indonesia's Riau-Lingga Archipelago and along the east coast of South Sumatra

The southern Malacca Strait region was historically one of the most pirate-prone in Southeast Asia. After the British and Dutch anti-piracy campaigns in the nineteenth century, however, piracy was all but exterminated in the area for more than a century. In contrast to the southern Philippines, where piracy surged immediately after World War II, the southern Malacca Strait region continued to be relatively free from pirates for several decades, even after the Dutch left their Indonesian colony in 1949, followed by the British in 1963.[26]

Piracy in the region only resurfaced on a significant scale in 1981. Excluding some cases of thefts in port, the first confirmed attack against a steaming vessel in the area in modern times occurred on 20 May 1981, when the Liberian flagged tanker *Koei* was boarded in the Phillip Channel. Over the following four months, another 21 attacks were reported in the Phillip Channel, in addition to a number of boardings of ships at anchor in or around Singapore harbour.[27] The attacks have continued up until today, even though the levels of activity have fluctuated drastically over the years, mostly due to the efforts on the part of the authorities in region to combat the problem. Many of the attacks occur in the congested Phillip Channel, where large vessels are forced to slow down, thus facilitating boarding for the pirates. Spates of attacks have also occurred further to the east, off Indonesia's Bintan Island, to the north, off the east coast of Indonesia's Riau province in the Strait of Malacca and around Indonesia's Natuna and Anambas Islands in the southwest South China Sea.

As for the other area in Southeast Asia where this type of piracy is rife today, around the islands of Bangka and Belitung off the coast of the Indonesian province of South Sumatra, the piratical activity

Map 4: South Malacca Strait area

appears to have started much later, around the mid-1990s. In numbers, the problem is smaller than in the Singapore Strait area, but the methods and objectives of the perpetrators are remarkably similar, suggesting, as we shall see, that there might be a connection between the two piracy 'hotspots'.

The low-level armed robberies, or 'petty piracy' attacks, are best described as quick hit-and-run operations. Most, but far from all, attacks occur at night, usually between midnight and 4 a.m., and most target ships are boarded while underway, sometimes at speeds of 15 knots or more. The pirates – normally a group of between four and ten men – approach their target from the stern in a small open craft generally powered by one or two powerful outboard engines that enable the pirate boat to do up to around 30–35 knots, or roughly about twice the cruising speed of most commercial vessels. The pirates often wear balaclavas over their heads or otherwise mask their faces to avoid recognition, and they are generally armed with simple weapons such as knives and machetes and sometimes firearms, but rarely automatic weapons.

Matching the speed of the larger ship, the pirates use grapnels, ropes, bamboo poles and other unsophisticated equipment to climb the hull at the stern – typically between three and five meters – up to the poop deck. While most of the pirates board the larger ship, one or two stay in the pirate boat being towed behind the target ship. Once on board the target vessel, the pirates aim not to be detected as they make their way inside the superstructure. They normally head for the master's cabin where the safe is located. If they cannot find the cabin, or if they are unable to make their way inside, they may instead head for the bridge, where they seize and threaten the officer-in-command, often leaving the ship steaming without command. They generally avoid injuring the prisoner or other crew members unless they meet with resistance. The pirates then proceed with their prisoner to the master's cabin, forcing him to open the safe or reveal where cash and valuables are kept. In some cases when the safe cannot be opened, the pirates have been known to steal the whole safe. The master's cabin may also be raided for more cash and personal belongings, and sometimes the pirates also loot the crew's quarters and the bridge. After seizing their loot the pirates make their way back to where they came from, disembark and take off. The whole attack will normally not last for more than 15–20 minutes, after which the pirates leave even if they fail to come over any booty. They may then move on to other targets, attacking up to three ships or even more in a single night's raiding.[28]

The target ships are of various types, including tugs and barges, bulk carriers, general cargo vessels, container ships and chemical as well as oil tankers, with gross tonnages ranging from as little as just over 100 tons to close to 70,000 (in 2004).[29] The flags of the target ships are from various countries in the region, including Indonesia, Malaysia and Singapore, and from others outside the region. Neither flag nor vessel type thus appears to be a major consideration for the pirates in their choice of target ships, even though some of the Indonesian perpetrators in the past have claimed never to attack Indonesian vessels[30] – probably, however, not so much out of patriotism as out of self-preservation. Size apparently only matters in that the largest ships, such as supertankers and other vessels with high freeboards, are avoided because of the difficulties in boarding them.[31]

The perpetrators of the low-level armed robberies take no interest in the ship's cargo, but instead primarily try to take cash and secondly easily portable and resaleable valuables. According to the victims' reports, cash amounts stolen generally range from a few hundred to a few thousand US dollars, even though several ships that were attacked in the early 1980s claimed to have been robbed of tens of thousands of dollars.[32] Apart from cash, other items that are frequently stolen include binoculars, cameras, audio-visual electronic equipment, clothing, credit cards, medicine and medical equipment, jewellery and watches.[33]

Who are these pirates that for more than two decades have harassed the crews and vessels passing through the Malacca and Singapore Straits and along the east coast of Sumatra? Most witness reports agree that they are Indonesians operating from Indonesian territory. As regards the attacks in and around the Singapore Strait, most, if not all, of the pirates are based in Indonesia's Riau archipelago, particularly in or around the island of Batam, some 10–15 kilometres south of Singapore. The island, which in the 1970s hosted but a few thousand people, mainly fishermen, has since the early 1980s been the scene of rapid economic development, providing the gradually more service-based Singaporean economy with an 'international hinterland with inexpensive labour', as the Swedish anthropologist Johan Lindquist has put it.[34] Attracted by Indonesia's low wages, relatively stable labour conditions and low taxes, around 1980 international companies began to establish manufacturing plants on the island, producing a variety of consumer goods such as clothes, shoes and electronics. Migrants from other parts of Indonesia, mainly Java and Sumatra, flocked to the island in search of work. In 1990, the idea was launched to create a quasi-official transnational economic growth triangle comprising Singapore, Batam and the Malaysian province of Johor north of Singapore, and throughout most of the 1990s, Batam witnessed a spectacular growth of manufacturing industries – as well as of tourism, entertainment and prostitution.

Many of the migrants who came to Batam after 1980 in search of jobs and opportunities, however, were unable to find work in line with their expectations and education, and many were unable to find any work at all. Young men often had more difficulties than young women to find jobs in the formal sector as many employers preferred female workers; they were regarded as more industrious and less likely to pose troublesome demands on the employer. Many men were thus forced to seek work in the informal sector, making their living as street vendors, motorcycle taxi drivers and touts, for example. Some also turned to criminal activities, including drug trafficking, procuring of sexual work, human smuggling, extortion, street robbery and theft. Piracy, in this context, appears to have been one of the options, especially for those who had some form of maritime experience and skills.

Data of arrested pirates from the Indonesian police in the first years of the 1990s indicate that most of the perpetrators of pirate attacks then were men in their thirties. Most also had secondary school education.[35] Not surprisingly, given the great influx of migrants to Riau, they were not natives of the archipelago but had moved there from other parts of Indonesia, including Sumatra, Java and Sulawesi. Coincidental or not, many of them seemed to come from the province of South Sumatra, the other major area of low-level armed robberies in Indonesia.[36]

The story of Syaiful Rozi bin Kahar, reported in 1993 by the Indonesian news magazine *Tempo*, may be illustrative of how some of the migrants to Batam ended up in the piracy business.[37] In 1981, Rozi, who was then 30 years old, came to Batam from his home village in South Sumatra to work at an electric appliance manufacturer where he had applied for a job. For some reason, however, he did not get the job and went instead to Malaysia where he worked illegally in a plantation for three months before being caught by the police and sent back to Indonesia. Back in Batam, he was introduced via a friend from his home province to a taxi boat driver, Abdul Rachman, who during day time took passengers short distances between the small islands of the archipelago. At night, Rachman supplemented his income from driving the taxi boat by raiding some of the hundreds of commercial vessels that each day passed through the Singapore Strait; via Rachman, Rozi was introduced to the trade. At first, his job was to bail water from the boat during raids, but as this only gave him a small share of the booty, he soon began to join the group of raiders who boarded the target ships. Rozi eventually advanced to become the leader of one of the major pirate gangs in Batam.

If the story in *Tempo* is correct, the sudden surge in piratical activity in the Phillip Channel in 1981 can be attributed to the activities of Rachman's group. According to the interview with Rozi, in the beginning the group consisted of only three men: Rachman, Mohammad Rasim and Adi Buldog [sic], who were what Rozi called the 'first generation' of modern pirates in Riau. Their *modus operandi* indicates that they had fairly detailed knowledge about the general design and conditions on board the target ships – especially concerning where they could expect to find cash and valuables. At least one of the pirates interviewed by *Tempo* in 1993 had worked as a crew member on international vessels before turning to piracy and could thus provide the necessary rudimentary intelligence for the first attacks.

Most of the pirates' nests in Riau were located in Belakang Padang, a district of small islands some 10–15 minutes by boat to the north-west of Batam's city centre. Close to the Phillip Channel with its busy international shipping lane, the islands of the Belakang Padang district are ideally located for piratical activity. One of the most infamous pirate islands, Amat Belanda, also known as Pulau Babi ('Pig Island'), is a brothel island catering mainly to male Singaporean weekend tourists.[38] This was where Rozi settled down and in time became a community leader of sorts, gaining a reputation among the residents of the island – most of whom were prostitutes – for being generous and helpful. Apart from freely lending and giving money to local residents in need, he financed the building of the island's first permanent mosque – located in the middle of the brothel area – and a footbridge connecting the island's residential-cum-brothel area with the boat landing.[39]

The Robin Hood image displayed by Rozi, however, is probably an exception to the rule. Most evidence – which admittedly is anecdotal – rather suggests that most of the proceedings from the raids are spent by the Batam pirates in less charitable ways, including the types of worldly pleasures normally associated with a buccaneering life style: drinking, gambling, prostitution and generally extravagant living. This is for example the impression gained by an encounter with the pirates on Pulau Babi reported in *Time* in 2001:

> The pirate king [...] stabs at his cellular phone, a huge gold and diamond band gilding his finger. Around a corner on the plank walkway, three men huddle over beer cans at a battered table, escaping the midday sun under a corrugated overhang. One of them looks up and breaks into a gold-plated grin. "Hey," he shouts. "I thought you were dead." [...] The pirate chiefs on Babi are old friends and have

> shared raids, women and tattoos. Like the pirate king, they are short, middle-aged and tanned. Their wiry arms speak of a physical working life, their beer bellies and mustaches of the nightclubs and bars it pays for.[40]

More recently, there appears to have been a generation shift among the pirates of Belakang Padang. According to Eric Frécon, who visited the area in 2004, many of the older pirates who were active already in the 1980s have retired from the business.[41] Rozi, meanwhile, appears to have been killed by a rival gang after talking to foreign journalists. Instead, younger men – including new recruits from South Sumatra who have come to Belakang Padang to 'be trained on the job' (as put by one of Frécon's informants) – have taken over.[42] The regrowth of the trade thus seems secured for the time being, and the petty pirate attacks are likely to continue in the region for the foreseeable future, unless the authorities find effective ways to curb their activities.

High-level armed robberies and kidnappings for ransom – the northern parts of the Malacca Strait

Just as in the southern parts of the Malacca Strait, piracy in the northern parts of the Strait was suppressed by the British and Dutch in the second half of the nineteenth century. During the Japanese occupation under World War II, however, piracy returned to the region on a significant scale, probably directly or indirectly triggered by the economic hardship and increased insecurity during the war years. As the British returned to the Malay Peninsula in August 1945, they found the northern parts of the Malacca Strait, particularly along the east coast close to the Thai border, rife with piracy, mainly affecting the local junk traffic. The problem grew worse towards the end of the year, prompting the British to launch a series of operations, lasting from December 1945 to March 1946, which cleared the pirates' land-bases on the islands of Langkawi and Tarutao.[43] After these operations, the northern parts of the Malacca Strait appear to have been virtually free from pirates until the end of the twentieth

Map 5: Malacca Strait and Sumatra

century. Even as piratical activity in the Singapore Strait and the southern parts of the Malacca Strait surged from the 1980s, the northern parts of the Malacca Strait – roughly north of the 3rd parallel North – continued to be safe.

This situation began to change in mid-2001, however, when the Indonesian-flagged tanker *Tirta Niaga IV* was attacked while anchored off the west coast of Aceh to conduct engine repairs. A group of pirates boarded the ship, robbed the crew and vessel of cash and valuables, and abducted the master and second officer. The second officer was released a few days later after negotiations, but the master was held hostage for more than six months before being released, reportedly after the Singaporean company that had chartered the vessel paid a US$ 30,000 ransom.[44]

The success of the first raid may well have encouraged more attacks in the area. In 2002, five attacks involving kidnappings were reported to the Piracy Reporting Centre of the International Maritime Bureau in Kuala Lumpur, and in 2003 there were four such attacks. In 2004 the number jumped to 14 – in addition to eight attempted attacks in which it was reported that vessels were fired at. The IMB, however, believes that these figures are only the tip of an iceberg as ship owners are reluctant to report the incidents and thereby risk the safety of the hostages. The ransoms demanded by the kidnappers, moreover, are usually quite 'reasonable' by international standards – typically a few thousand dollars for each person – which probably encourages ship owners to meet the demands of the kidnappers rather than report the matter to the police or other authorities.[45]

The attacks in the northern parts of the Malacca Strait are characterised by higher levels of violence and greater ruthlessness than those in the southern parts of the Strait. The pirates are almost invariably armed with firearms, often automatic weapons, and sometimes with other heavy weapons as well, such as grenades. Pirates often fire at vessels in order to make them stop, thereby putting both the vessel and crew at serious risk. The most brutal incident so far occurred on 5 January 2004 when the Indonesian oil tanker *Cherry 201* was hijacked off the north coast of Aceh. The pirates took the 13 crew members hostage, but released the captain so that he could convey their demand for ransom. The kidnappers initially demanded 400 million Indonesian Rupiah (Rp) (US$ 47,616) for the release of the hostages, but the owners of the vessel, an Indonesian palm oil company, negotiated the ransom down to a quarter of the original amount. When the owners tried to bargain further, however, the kidnappers, one month after the hijacking, lost patience and shot dead four of the Indonesian crew members. The remaining 12 jumped overboard and escaped.[46]

Most of the attacks in the northern parts of the Malacca Strait over the past four years have occurred in the far north-western parts of the Strait, mainly close to the Acehnese coast, and hostages tend to have been held captive in Aceh. Some attacks have also taken place further to the south, off the coast of the Indonesian province of North Sumatra and, in a few cases, closer to the Malaysian side of the Strait. The victims of the kidnapping attacks are not only commercial vessels and their crews, but also local fishing and trading boats. In the first two weeks of August 2002, six Indonesian fishing boats with 46 crew members were hijacked, and the pirates reportedly demanded Rp 800 million (c. US$ 88,000) for the release of each vessel.[47] The IMB has also reported several brutal attacks on Malaysian fishing boats in the northern Malacca Strait, even though many such attacks probably have gone unreported.[48] In May 2004, the director of the North Sumatra Fishery Office, Ridwan Batubara, claimed that at least 30 vessels, including 15 Indonesian fishing boats, had been attacked off the coast of Aceh and North Sumatra in the first four months of the year. He also estimated that 8,000 fishing boats – two-thirds of the province's fishing fleet – were not operating because of the threat of piracy.[49]

Criminal groups in the area also extort money from fishermen. In January 2003, the *Jakarta Post* quoted a North Sumatra businessman who owned a number of fishing vessels saying that different groups of armed pirates would demand between Rp 1 and 2 million (c. US$ 110–220) each in protection money, and that sometimes vessels had to pay up to Rp 4 million (c. US$ 450) on one day for all the groups they came across.[50]

In the wake of the tsunami that on 26 December 2004 laid most of Aceh's coastal areas in ruins, piracy in the region ceased completely, and for two months there were no reported attacks in the northern parts of the Malacca Straits.[51] The reasons are not difficult to imagine. Several of the Acehnese pirates are likely to have been killed by the wave, and those who survived probably had much of their equipment, including boats, engines and weapons, destroyed. The lull, however, was temporary. From the end of February 2005, piratical activity resumed off the Acehnese coast, still characterised by shootings, kidnappings and generally high levels of violence.

Because several of the incidents have occurred close to the coast of Aceh, suspicions have been raised that the perpetrators have been members of the Free Aceh Movement, GAM (Gerakan Aceh Merdeka), which since 1976 has fought an armed battle for Acehnese independence from Indonesia. Allegations of GAM involvement in the pirate attacks, however, have mainly come from the Indonesian military and need to be treated with caution. For example, Indonesian military sources claimed that the hijackers of a Honduran-flagged tug boat, *Ocean Silver*, in August 2001, demanded a ransom of Rp 300 million (c. US$ 33,000) from the ship owner as a financial contribution for the struggle for Aceh's independence.[52] However, a GAM spokesman, Ishak Daud, denied that the organisation had anything to do with the kidnappings and claimed instead that the incident had been staged by the Indonesian military in order to make GAM look like terrorists in the eyes of the international community. 'How could we have pirated that ship when the waters of Aceh are daily crawling with war vessels of the Indonesian navy which has stepped up its patrols?' he rhetorically asked reporters.[53]

Another attack which the Indonesian authorities blamed on GAM was the hijacking of the Indonesian fishing boat *Champion* with 11 crew members on 10 February 2004. According to the IMB, the boat was hijacked by a group of three pirates in the waters off Tanjung Balai Asahan near the North Sumatran port of Belawan, but according to the Indonesian navy the incident took place near the Berhala Islands near the Acehnese coast. Acting on intelligence, an Indonesian naval vessel reportedly ordered the ship to stop, but as the pirates refused, an exchange of gunfire ensued. The hijackers continued to defy the orders of the naval vessel, and the confrontation only ended after the navy fired on the hijacked vessel, causing it to sink. The eleven crew members and three pirates were rescued by the Indonesian naval vessel, and the three pirates, claimed by the

Indonesian military to be GAM rebels, were then paraded, blindfolded, before press cameras in the North Aceh regency capital, Lhokseumawe.[54]

On the basis of the testimonies of released hostages, the IMB also believes that GAM may have been involved in the kidnapping attacks in the northern parts of the Malacca Strait in recent years. The director of the Bureau's Piracy Reporting Centre in Kuala Lumpur, Noel Choong, however, acknowledges that the attacks may also be the doings of common bandits with little political or ideological motivation.[55] The latter view is supported by a recent analysis of GAM by Kirsten Schulze of Washington's East–West Center. According to Schulze, piracy does not really fit GAM's *modus operandi* and is more likely to be a 'product of warlordism and the result of local decision making'.[56] The political leaders of the organisation, most of whom reside in Sweden, have in recent years worked hard and consistently to gain the support of the international community for their cause, and endorsing piratical activity would be clearly detrimental to this strategy.

On 15 August 2005, representatives of the Indonesian government and the Free Aceh Movement signed a peace agreement in Helsinki which, if successfully implemented, will put an end to nearly three decades of hostilities in the province. In the short term, however, the agreement failed to put an end to the piratical activity off the Acehnese coast. Within two weeks of the signing of the agreement, there were three attacks – two of which involved kidnappings – against Indonesian vessels off the east coast of the province, and the Indonesian military again claimed that they were perpetrated by GAM rebels.[57] With GAM still officially supporting the peace accord and with disarmament of the organisation's guerrilla fighters continuing, it seems even more unlikely than in the past that these attacks were endorsed by the GAM leaders. The continuing piratical activity off the Acehnese coast instead strengthens suspicions that the attacks are carried out by local bandits, possibly posing as GAM rebels, or by loose bands of GAM supporters acting independently of the organisation. The peace agreement is unlikely to put an end to the activities of such groups, and if law and order is effectively restored in the province, it may actually trigger an increase in piratical activity as outlaw elements seek alternative incomes.

❧

In spite of the characterisations of maritime Southeast Asia as 'pirate infested' and of piracy as 'endemic' to the region,[58] it is only a problem in three relatively limited parts of the region. In the first of these, the Sulu region of the southern Philippines and eastern Malaysia, piracy started already in the aftermath of World War II, triggered by the proliferation of small arms and US surplus engines, both of which provided the pirates with the necessary tools for their activities. Piratical activity was also encouraged by a historical and cultural sanctioning of such activities among some of the seafaring communities in the area, for instance the Tausug and Samal of Jolo and Tawi-tawi. In this context, the motives may, at least among some of the perpetrators, have been as much social as economic in that maritime raiding was (and is) associated with risk taking and male prowess. Such cultural sanctioning of piratical activity together with the proliferation of firearms in the region has acted to increase the levels of violence, probably making the the waters of the southern Philippines and adjacent eastern Malaysia the most dangerous and pirate infested region in the world today. The victims of the violence are not so much international shipping but local seafarers, including fishermen and sea nomads, and coastal dwellers.

Separately, sustained piratical activity emerged in the southern parts of the Malacca Strait and the Singapore Strait in 1981. In contrast to the Sulu region, there is no evidence of a cultural or historical continuity between the pirate communities who raided ships in the area up until the second half of the nineteenth century and those who do so today. The contemporary pirates seem mainly to be migrants to the area, coming from different, often distant, parts of Indonesia, including Java, Sumatra and Sulawesi. Moreover, in contrast to the situation in the southern Philippines, the Indonesian pirates operating in the southern Malacca Strait region do not appear to come from ethnic groups that are weakly integrated in the nation – even though they may be relatively socially and economically disadvantaged.

Broadly speaking, the roots of contemporary piracy in the southern Malacca Strait region can be found in the rapid social and economic change, due to the expansion of global capitalism that over the past decades has affected the region and which is particularly obvious in the spectacular growth of Batam on the southern side of the Singapore Strait. The pirates' motives are more straightforwardly pecuniary compared with in the southern Philippines, and there is no evidence of a broader cultural sanctioning of piracy (that is, outside the pirates' immediate social group) or any association between piracy and highly regarded male virtues such as honour, bravery and masculinity. Violence, in this context, has no self-serving purpose but tends to be used more sparingly and generally only as a means of coercion. Firearms are also much less widely available in the southern Malacca Strait region than in the southern Philippines, and to the extent that pirates are armed with guns these tend to be non-automatic and quite seldom used.

Several of the pirates operating out of Batam over the past decades have come from the Indonesian province of South Sumatra, and it is possible that piratical activity in that area, which started around 1995, is linked through personal networks to the activity in the southern Malacca Strait region. The probability of a link between the piratical activities in the two regions is strengthened by the similarity in the *modus operandi* of the South Sumatra pirates and their colleagues in the southern Malacca Strait region. Piratical activity in both regions is what may be termed 'petty piracy', taking the form of brief 'hit-and-run' robberies of commercial vessels, generally involving low levels of violence.

The last region in which opportunistic piracy has resumed in recent years is the northern parts of the Malacca Strait, particularly off the coast of the Indonesian province of Aceh. Piratical activity there tends to be more violent than in the southern parts of the Strait and often involves the use of automatic weapons by perpetrators who seem to have little regard for the life and safety of their victims. Much of the maritime violence is obviously linked to the unrest and insecurity in Aceh with local criminal groups – some of which may be associated with, or posing as members of, the Free Aceh Movement – conducting kidnappings of crew members and fishermen for ransom. This type of attacks only started in 2001, two decades after the first surge in contemporary piracy in the southern parts of the Strait.

Different as the three main types of opportunistic piracy in Southeast Asia are in terms of the underlying economic, social and cultural motivations, the levels and types of violence used, the type of victims, objectives and *modus operandi* of the pirates, they are united by one crucial factor which provides the opportunity for pirates to attack their prey, namely speed. Already after World War II, the availability of American surplus outboard engines in the Sulu region gave pirates there the means and equipment with which to overtake their victims at sea. Likewise, in the Strait of Malacca (as elsewhere), commercially produced outboard engines became both more powerful and economically more viable from the 1970s. Even simple open wooden boats could be equipped with two, and sometimes three, powerful outboard engines, giving the pirate a decisive superiority over their victims – be they commercial vessels, fishing boats or pleasure yachts – in terms of speed and manoeuvrability. This not only meant that they could easily overtake their victims but also that they could quickly escape after an attack. The relative superiority in terms of speed and manoeuvrability are advantages which today's opportunistic pirates in Southeast Asia share with several of history's most successful raiders around the world, including the Vikings of ninth- and tenth-century Northern Europe, the galley-equipped Barbary pirates of the sixteenth-, seventeenth- and eighteenth-century Mediterranean and the feared Illanun slave raiders in Southeast Asia in the first half of the nineteenth century.

Notes

1 This type of attack has been so prevalent over the past decades as to lead some observers to call them 'Asian' piracy; e.g. ICC International

Maritime Bureau (1998b: 7). This description, however, is unfortunate, and even misleading, since it only fits one of the major types of piracies that occur in Asia.

2 'United States of America Philippine Islands in the Supreme Court of the Philippine Islands in Banc. The People of the Philippines, plaintiff and Appellee, Vs. Lol-o and Saraw, Defendants and Appellants', ARA, MvBZ, A-dossiers, A134, nr 1123 (27 February 1922). The case is interesting from a legal perspective because the Supreme Court, referring to piracy as a crime against all mankind and pirates as *hostis humani generis*, claimed that it was within its jurisdiction even though the attack took place in Dutch territorial waters; see further Rubin (1998: 347).

3 Kiefer (1972: 4).

4 [British Legation Manila to the Foreign Office], NA, FO 371/84337 (24 July 1950).

5 Hedman and Sidel (2000: 170). For the connection between the barter trade and piratical activity in the region in the 1950s and early 1960s, see Eklöf (2005).

6 *Beloy Montemayor* and *Montemayor: Tulisang Dagat* ('Montemayor: The sea robber'); see Sidel (1995: 149).

7 Ibid. (1995: 148–168).

8 'Piracies and armed raids', note attached to [The Governor of North Borneo to the Secretary of the State for the Colonies], NA, CO 1030/1660 (8 January 1963). See also Eklöf (2005).

9 'Armed raids along the Coastline of North Borneo' [Acting Governor of North Borneo to the Commander-in-Chief, Far East Station], NA, DO 169/31 (30 July 1962).

10 Warren (2002: 379).

11 Ikuya Tokoro, who did fieldwork among the Samal of Tawi-tawi in the 1990s, confirms that the piratical raids of their nineteenth-century forefathers were still in living memory among the Samal and contributed to sanction piratical activity in modern times; oral presentation at the workshop on "Ports, Pirates and Hinterlands in East and Southeast Asia", organised by the Shanghai Academy of Social Sciences and the Center for Maritime Research (MARE), University of Amsterdam, Shanghai, 11 November 2005.

12 See *Asiaweek* (21 April 1993), Aschan (1996: 49), Sather (1997: 104) and Warren (2003: 18).

13 Kiefer (1972: 85).

14 Ibid. (1972: 85). Kiefer uses the term 'minimal alliance group' to describe such armed bands. A minimal alliance group can occasionally form temporary alliances with other groups, thus forming so-called 'medial alliance groups'; ibid. (1972: 71–73).

15 Ibid. (1972: 83–84). Similar social and cultural sanctions for various kinds of outlaw behaviour can apparently also be found among the Yakan in western Mindanao; see Frake (1998: 48).

16 Sather (1997: 104).

17 *Asiaweek* (21 April 1993).

18 A recent study of small arms production and transfers in Southeast Asia noted that the Philippines is a 'heavily armed society, with a level of civilian gun ownership close to that of the United States'; Capie (2002: 67). See also ibid. (2002: 73–74) and the discussion about the involvement of insurgent groups in piratical activity in the region in Chapter 7.

19 *Asiaweek* (21 April 1993).

20 'Piracy and Armed Robbery against Ships. South China Sea. Report on IMO's fact-finding mission. Note by the Secretariat', IMO, MCS 63/INF.15 (25 March 1994), item 49.

21 Santos (2004: 3).

22 See, e.g. *Asiaweek* (27 May 1988); see also the information provided by the Philippine Coast Guard on the issue of missing victims of pirate attacks in 'Piracy and armed robbery against ships. South China Sea: Report on IMO's fact-finding mission. Note by the Secretariat', IMO MSC 63/INF.15 (25 March 1994), item 40.

23 Ibid., items 43 and 47.

24 *Asiaweek* (27 May 1988).

25 Abhyankar (2002: 14).

26 The piratical activity which did occur during the 1950s and 1960s seems to have been perpetrated by Indonesian regular and irregular forces and linked to international maritime and political disputes, including Indonesia's policy of Confrontation against Malaysia. The British reported that Indonesian troops regularly committed pirate attacks against Malaysian fishing vessels in the 1950s; see [Commander-in-Chief, Far Eastern Station to Admiralty], NA, AIR 2/12136 (20 November 1953), and in 1963, shortly after Malaysian independence, the country's Prime Minister Tungku Abdul Rahman complained over

attacks by the Indonesian navy against Malaysian fishing boats; see his speech before the Malaysian Parliament in Bastin and Winks (eds) (1966: 436).

27 The attack on the *Koei* is the first confirmed attack against a steaming vessel in the region listed both by the first report to the IMO on the matter and by Villar (1985: 118). For the IMO report, which was prepared by the International Maritime Bureau, see 'A report into the incidence of Piracy and Armed Robbery from merchant ships', IMO MSC 48/INF.6 (6 June 1983). The two lists of attacks appear, at least in part, two be compiled from different sources, Villar's list being the more complete.

28 This description is based on a report in the Indonesian news magazine *Tempo* (28 August 1993), which provides a detailed description of the *modus operandi* of some of the Riau pirates.

29 The smallest vessel reported by the IMB to have sustained a low-level armed robbery in the southern Malacca Straits in 2004 was the tug *Aqua Perdana* (131 tons) and the largest was the bulk carrier *Cape Haralambos* (69,234 tons); ICC – International Maritime Bureau (2005a: 30, 40).

30 *Tempo* (28 August 1993).

31 The 1983 IMB report to the IMO observed: 'Many of the vessels attacked are laden tankers or similar vessels whose low freeboard makes them easy to board using grappling irons, even whilst travelling at relatively high speeds of up to twelve knots'; 'A report into the incidence of piracy and armed robbery from merchant ships', IMO MSC 48/INF.6 (6 June 1983), p. 6.

32 In the first years of the 1980s, the highest figure, US$ 50,000, was reported by the Panamanian-registered bulk carrier *Hand Ming*, which was attacked outside of Singapore on 29 October 1982; see Villar (1985: 124). See further the discussion on the costs of piracy in Chapter 6 below.

33 Villar (1985: 118–130).

34 Lindquist (2002: 10); see also ibid. (2002: 63–68) about the development of Batam.

35 *Kompas* (4 November 1992).

36 Of the six pirates who were convicted in Riau for piracy between January and November 1992, four were from South Sumatra; *Kompas* (4 November 1992). Likewise, a feature in Time (Asian Internet edition)

(20 August 2001) nine years later claimed that most of the pirates then active on Pulau Babi were from the South Sumatran capital of Palembang.

37 *Tempo* (28 August 1993).

38 Most of the pirates that were arrested when the Indonesian authorities cracked down on the pirates from mid-1992 were caught on Pulau Babi; see *Merdeka* (9 November 1992).

39 See *Tempo* (28 August 1993).

40 *Time* (Asian Internet edition) (20 August 2001).

41 Frécon (2006).

42 Ibid. From his life story, the pirate leader identified by Frécon as 'Nasrul' appears to be identical to the person identified as 'Rozi' by *Tempo*.

43 'Operations of Penang Sub-Area and 74th Indian Infantry Brigade in the suppression of piracy off the west coast of Malaya and Siam, December 1945–March 1946', NA, WO 203/6268 (April 1946). See also Miller (1970) for some notes on piracy in the region in the immediate post-war years.

44 ICC – International Maritime Bureau (2002: 19) and Burnett (2002: 324).

45 Interview with the regional director of the Piracy Reporting Centre of the IMB, Noel Choong, Kuala Lumpur, 16 January 2004. See also ICC – International Maritime Bureau (2003: 26–47 and 2004: 27–44).

46 *Jakarta Post* (6 February 2004).

47 *Kompas* (14 August 2002). See also *New Straits Times* (4 November 2003) about attacks against Malaysian fishermen from Hutan Melintang in southern Perak.

48 See, e.g. ICC – International Maritime Bureau (2004: 18) and (2005a: 17).

49 *Jakarta Post* (10 May 2004).

50 Ibid. (13 January 2003).

51 See 'Reports on acts of piracy and armed robbery against ships. Issued monthly – Acts reported during January 2005', IMO MSC.4/Circ 65 (14 March 2005) and 'Reports on acts of piracy and armed robbery against ships. Issued monthly – Acts reported during February 2005', IMO MSC.4/Circ.66 (15 April 2005) for reported incidents during January and February 2005.

52 *Kompas* (30 August 2001).

53 Agence France Presse (3 September 2001). Obviously contradicting himself, however, he also claimed that only GAM – and not the Indonesian navy – was able to secure Malacca Straits for shipping. Moreover, Ishak indicated that GAM might have some responsibility for the attack, saying: 'If they [shippers] do not want to seek permission from us, then they should not blame the GAM if cases such as experienced by the Honduran-flagged Ocean Silver ship repeat itself again.'

54 ICC – International Maritime Bureau (2005: 31) and *Jakarta Post* (14 February 2004).

55 Interview by the author, Kuala Lumpur, 16 January 2004. IMB Director P. Mukundan (2004: 4) likewise concluded that the attack on the Malaysian tanker *Penrider* in August 2003 may have been conducted by 'criminals posting as GAM rebels'.

56 Schulze (2004: 28).

57 Antara (1 September 2005).

58 E.g. Young (2005: 16).

CHAPTER 5

Phantom Ships and Organised Crime

LEGEND HAS IT that in the 1980s, Captain Emilio Chengco, one of the most notorious pirates of the Philippines, used to take his clients to the sky bar in the Hilton Bayview Park Hotel in Manila. Pointing at the myriad of ships at anchor in Manila Bay, Captain Chengco would ask: 'Which one of these would you like?'

Carrying out hijackings to order, Emilio Chengco was the leader of a criminal syndicate that in the late 1980s and early 1990s was responsible for a spate of hijackings of commercial vessels in the Philippines. According to information obtained by the International Maritime Bureau, a ship could be hijacked in the Philippines for about US$ 300,000 and be delivered within three days.[1]

Even though the operations of Captain Chengco ceased at the beginning of the 1990s – he was arrested in 1992 and subsequently reportedly killed when he tried to escape from a high-security prison in Manila[2] – hijackings by organised crime syndicates in East and Southeast Asia continue to be a serious problem for the shipping industry. The problem was particularly acute in the second half of the 1990s, when several highly published and often violent cases of hijackings of commercial vessels occurred. The attacks against commercial vessels in Southeast Asia decreased sharply in the early 2000s but organised pirates in the region have instead increasingly begun to attack soft targets such as tugs and barges. In spite of the relatively small number of such incidents compared with the large increase in opportunistic piracy, they seem to be of more serious concern for the shipping industry because of both the high levels of violence often directed at crews and the greater economic losses involved.

Hijackings of commercial vessels obviously involve a great deal more in terms of planning and sophistication than most of the locally perpetrated attacks that have been described so far. Compared with the opportunistic piracy described in the previous chapter, the organised and carefully planned hijacking of whole vessels is a relatively recent development, the roots of which can be traced to three other, interrelated forms of maritime crime preceding it by at least some decades. These are insurance fraud, documentary fraud and cargo diversion.[3]

There are two main types of maritime insurance fraud: cargo fraud, in which indemnity is claimed for an allegedly stolen, substituted or non-existent cargo, and hull fraud, in which a vessel is 'scuttled' – that is, deliberately sunk – or otherwise made to disappear in order for the fraudster to be able to collect the insurance money. After having been a relatively minor concern for the East Asian insurance companies in the 1950s and 1960s, the instances of suspected fraud in East Asian waters increased dramatically in the second half of the 1970s, giving rise to suspicions that one or several ship-sinking syndicates were responsible. In 1979, after more than 40 suspicious incidents resulted in claims of more than US$ 100 million in two years, a number of insurance companies agreed to set up the Far Eastern Regional Investigation Team (FERIT) in order to enquire into these losses and to further investigate the reports that an organised criminal group was behind the wave of reported losses. The team's report – which was confidential but the main findings of which were widely circulated and published – supported the theory that there indeed existed a widespread and highly organised maritime insurance fraud industry in Eastern Asia. The team found that several companies and individuals appeared in more than one of the suspected cases. Often, the ship-owners and crew members had links to the Chinese Nationalist Party, Guomindang, in Taiwan. Apparently, some were specialists in sinking ships, the *Far Eastern Economic Review* noting they had 'spent more time queuing for lifeboats than sitting for licence examinations'. FERIT also found that there was some evidence that the ship-sinking syndicates were involved in drug trafficking and smuggling of refugees, particularly from Vietnam.[4]

Often, the suspected incidents included both cargo and hull fraud. The following story of how a cargo of high-value eels destined for the Japanese market were diverted, reported by the *Far Eastern Economic Review* in 1979, provides an example of the operations:

> According to sources [in the insurance industry], the eels are loaded on a Taiwan vessel bound for Japan. The ship meets a Taiwan-based trawler at sea, unloads the cargo and proceeds to a spot off the Japanese coast, where it is scuttled. The eels are brought back into Taiwan as the trawler's catch, thus avoiding import duties, and the payments on the hull and cargo are collected from the Japanese insurers.
>
> The strength of this method of fraud is that the proceeds from the sale of the eels are almost immediate, thus alleviating the cash flow problem that has led so many crews spilling details of schemes to insurers. Scuttling crews normally expect an immediate pay-off. In aggregate this would often amount to 15% of the insured value of the hull and the cargo.[5]

The FERIT report alerted insurance companies as well as authorities in the region to the problem of maritime insurance fraud and thus probably contributed to a considerable decline in the number of such incidents in the early 1980s. Contributing to the decline in maritime insurance fraud was also the initiative by the International Chamber of Commerce to set up the International Maritime Bureau (IMB) in 1981. The IMB was specifically charged with the task of countering maritime fraud and related crimes.[6]

Even though the number of suspected insurance frauds declined, there were, as Jayant Abhyankar of the IMB has observed, few criminal prosecutions as a result of the FERIT report.[7] Most of the perpetrators consequently remained at large and were free to divert their energies to other types of maritime crime. Consequently, it seems that in the first half of the 1980s documentary fraud succeeded insurance fraud as the maritime crime in East Asia which was of most concern to the shipping industry. Documentary fraud involves forged or false documents, usually bills of lading, certificates of origin or commercial invoices. The buyer pays upon receiving the documents, but the cargo is never loaded on the vessel or named on the bill of lading, or is substituted for a cargo of scrap. When the buyer discovers the fraud, the seller has simply disappeared or gone into liquidation.[8]

In the mid-1980s, organised maritime crime in East and Southeast Asia took yet one step further, as systematic diversion of cargo, involving the use of so-called 'phantom ships', began to be reported. A phantom ship is a falsely registered ship that is used by a criminal group to take up cargoes that are never delivered to the proper destination. Instead, the ship is diverted, provided with a false new identity, and the cargo sold to a third party. The ship's identity is then again altered and the fraud can be repeated by taking on new cargo assignments. An illustration is the fate of the *Silver Med*, a Liberian-registered 5,350-ton vessel that was hijacked – most likely, by Emilio Chengco's group – in Manila Bay on 13 September 1988. Two weeks after she was hijacked, the ship was reportedly sighted in international waters outside Singapore under the name of *Lambamba*. The vessel was then renamed again, and as the *Sea Rex*, she loaded a cargo of plywood, bound for Huang Pu, China, in the Indonesian port of Samarinda. The cargo, however, was diverted and taken to Zamboanga in the southern Philippines, where it was unlawfully sold. By January 1989, the ship appeared in Malaysia and Singapore, now under the name of *Stamford*, where she loaded steel, palm oil, stearin and natural rubber bound for China and Hong Kong. The cargo was again diverted to the Philippines, where the ship – now renamed the *Star Ace* – was finally intercepted by Philippine customs and the crew was arrested.[9]

Although the syndicates may sometimes acquire phantom ships in legal ways, many of them are hijacked in carefully planned and organised operations. For example, of the seven vessels hijacked in the Philippines between 1986 and 1989, at least three – including the

Silver Med – were found to be used by criminal syndicates for illicit purposes. False registration of phantom ships is facilitated by the lax standards and lack of control on the part of the ship registries of certain flag states, including Honduras and Panama. According to the IMB, corrupt officials of these and other countries may, for a fee that is several times higher than the normal fee, issue temporary registrations based on false information concerning the ship's previous names, tonnages, dimensions and ownership.[10] In this way, a phantom ship can avoid being recognised even if an international warrant had been issued. Moreover, even if arrested, the multiple false registrations make it extremely difficult for the authorities and other interested parties to trace the vessel's movements prior to its interception.

About the time of the arrest of Emilio Chengco in 1992, organised piracy shifted to other parts of East and Southeast Asia. The first reported case in the Malacca Strait area, for example, occurred in August 1991, when the *Sprintstar* was attacked by 25 armed pirates eight kilometres east of Singapore. The pirates fatally wounded the chief officer and handcuffed the crew for two days, as the ship's entire cargo, reportedly worth US$ 3 million, was stolen and transferred to another ship.[11] In December the following year, the *Far Trader*, a 500-ton vessel carrying a cargo of textiles, food, electronic goods and cigarettes destined for Okinawa, was attacked near Indonesia's Natuna Islands in the South China Sea. A group of masked pirates armed with automatic weapons fired on the ship before they boarded and took control over the vessel. The crew were locked in the engine room while the pirates ransacked the ship and dismantled all radio and navigational equipment. The ship was then diverted to Thailand, where the cargo – valued at more than US$ 7 million – was transferred to another ship which came alongside.[12]

According to the IMB, there were no hijackings in 1993, but over the following four years, between 1994 and 1997, the Bureau recorded nine hijackings of commercial vessels in East and Southeast Asian waters.[13] Most of the targets were either tankers or general cargo vessels of small or medium size. The hijackings occurred in different parts of the area: three took place south of Hong Kong, three in the

Gulf of Thailand, two in the Singapore Strait area, and one in Vietnamese waters. In most cases, the hijacked vessel was diverted to a port in south China, such as Shanwei, Beihai or Hui Lai, where the cargo (and in some instances the vessel as well) was disposed of. Several of the hijackings involved what appeared to be Chinese military or customs personnel and equipment, and the subsequent fate of several of the ships, cargoes and crews in Chinese ports indicated that some officials colluded with the pirates. The case of the *Anna Sierra* in 1995, is one of the best-documented and most-illustrative cases of the type of organised piracy in Southeast Asia in the 1990s. In contrast to most hijackings, however, the plot was revealed and the ship was located – something which makes it possible to reconstruct the scheme behind the event.[14]

On 12 September, the Cyprus-registered bulk carrier *Anna Sierra* left Ko Si Chang, southeast of Bangkok, bound for Manila. On board, she carried a crew of 23 and a cargo of 12,000 tons of sugar worth US$ 5 million. Shortly after midnight on 13 September the *Anna Sierra* was proceeding south in the Gulf of Thailand when she was attacked by 30 pirates armed with submachine guns. After boarding the ship, the pirates handcuffed the crew and locked them in two small cabins. Two days later, off the south Vietnamese coast, the crew was forced off the ship in two life rafts. They were rescued later the same day by Vietnamese fishermen. Around half of the pirate gang left the ship on the motor boat which they had used for boarding the ship, taking cash and valuables with them. Left on board were 14 of the pirates acting as crew.

The *Anna Sierra* then proceeded north to the Chinese port of Beihai in Guanxi province, where she arrived on 20 September, one week after the hijacking. The ship had now been renamed the *Artic Sea* [sic] and provided with false documents from the Honduras Registry of Shipping. Apparently, the pirates intended to unload the cargo of sugar in Beihai; it later transpired that a trader in Beihai had ordered the shipment in early September, that is, already before the *Anna Sierra* was hijacked. For unknown reasons, however, the cargo was not unloaded. The ship was instead detained by Chinese Frontier

Defence Authority (Banfong) which put two armed guards on board and seized the ship's documents and the passports of the crew.

At the beginning of October, investigators of the IMB, which had been contacted by the shipowner after the ship had been hijacked, arrived in Beihai and were able positively to identify the ship as the *Anna Sierra*. Eventually, in December, the Chinese authorities recognised that the ship was in fact the *Anna Sierra* but nevertheless refused to return the ship to the shipowner, claiming that they were still investigating the case. However, none of the detained crew members was formally interviewed by China's Public Security Bureau (PSB) the authority in charge of the investigation.

In February 1996, the PSB offered to release the ship provided the shipowner paid a fee of US$ 400,000 to the Bureau for its costs and other expenses. As the shipowner refused to pay, however, the ship remained in Beihai, where its maintenance was neglected. In July, the crew of pirates was taken off the ship – they were subsequently repatriated to their countries of origin with no legal prosecu-tion – and the ship was left unmanned. In early 1997, the PSB noticed that the ship's engine room and holds were partially flooded with sea water, and the cargo was discharged to a warehouse. As the *Anna Sierra* continued to take in sea water and developed a ten degree list, the port authorities decided to tow her to a nearby beach. In August, the PSB auctioned the cargo without consulting the owners.

Apart from the obvious uncooperative stance of the Chinese authorities in handling the *Anna Sierra* case, several cases in the 1990s also strongly indicated that some Chinese law enforcement officials directly perpetrated pirate attacks against commercial vessels in the waters of China's eastern and southern coasts. According to press reports, citing a report issued by the government of Hong Kong, Chinese security forces and government officials were implicated in some 42 incidents in 1993–1994. Some of these included eye-witnesses positively identifying customs, naval and police officers through the serial numbers of the patrol vessels involved.[15]

The incidents had various characteristics and occurred both in Chinese territorial waters and in international waters. Sometimes, the intercepted vessel was allowed to proceed after paying fines of up to US$ 150,000 but in other cases the ship was forced into a Chinese harbour where the crew would be arrested and charged with smuggling. In 1995, for example, the *Hye Mieko* was intercepted off Cambodia, reportedly by a 'boat resembling a Chinese customs launch'.[16] The vessel was forced with its cargo of cigarettes to the Guangdong port of Shanwei, east of Hong Kong, where the crew was arrested and charged with attempting to smuggle cigarettes into China. The cargo was confiscated and sold by the authorities.

Some observers have suggested that the involvement of Chinese officials in piratical incidents may, as put by Peter Chalk, have been part of a 'deliberate exercise [on the part of Beijing] of extra-territorial sovereignty through a *de facto* exertion of expansive maritime claims in the South China Sea'.[17] By and large, however, the involvement of Chinese officials in piracy can also be explained by the wide-spread corruption in official circles in the mid-1990s. The combination of high demand and various restrictions on the import of raw materials, such as rubber and petrochemicals, as well as consumer goods like cigarettes, electronics and cars, created a favourable environment for smuggling and other forms of illicit trade. Officials in the navy, police and customs authorities were well placed to take advantage of this situation and, for the most part, the involvement of certain officials in piratical incidents can probably be attributed to the widespread corruption.

Although details are largely lacking, there are clear indications that the corruption in official Chinese circles was linked to transnational organised criminal activities, including those of a number of international syndicates that were responsible for most, if not all, hijackings of commercial ships in East and Southeast Asian waters in the 1990s. According to the IMB, four major syndicates had by the end of the 1990s divided maritime East and Southeast Asia between them. The syndicates, all of which conducted hijackings and operated phantom ships in the region, were organised along ethnic lines with three Chinese gangs – one each from Guangzhou (Canton), Fujian and Shanghai – in East and Southeast Asia and one Indian syndicate mainly working in the Andaman Sea.[18] The Chinese syndicates were reportedly controlled by a small number of highly experienced businessmen operating out of Hong Kong, Indonesia, the Philippines and Thailand. Although several of the syndicate members – some of whom were involved in the insurance frauds in the 1970s and figured already in the FERIT report – were well known to law enforcement authorities in the region, they could not be prosecuted due to lack of evidence. Further complicating action against them was that they had good connections to members of the governments in the region, including, as euphemistically put by the IMB, 'one of the Royal Families of the area'.[19]

From an average of around two hijackings per year in the mid-1990s, the activity of the syndicates surged in 1998 – possibly as a result of declining business opportunities in other sectors in the wake of the Asian economic crisis the year before. In 1998 alone, the IMB recorded seven cases of hijackings of commercial vessels in East and Southeast Asian waters. Of these, the best-documented was the hijacking of the *Petro Ranger* in April 1998.[20] The case is also illustrative, as it obviously involved both organised criminals and official corruption.

At 4.15 p.m. on 16 April 1998, the 128-metre tanker vessel *Petro Ranger* left Singapore with a cargo of 9,600 tons of automotive diesel oil and 1,600 tons of jet fuel worth around US$ 1.5 million bound for Saigon. Nine hours later, while underway off the east coast of peninsular Malaysia, the ship was boarded by a group of 12 pirates armed with guns, machetes and knives. The crew of 23 was rounded up and locked in the mess while the *Petro Ranger* was diverted towards the south China coast. Meanwhile, the ship's name was painted out and substituted with the name *Wilby* in the ship's bow and stern as well as on all life jackets and equipment. The pirates also had false registration documents for the *Wilby*, issued five weeks before the hijacking by the Philippine consulate of Honduras.

On 22 April, some 230 kilometres off the coast of Hainan, much of the cargo of diesel oil was discharged into two smaller tankers that were brought alongside the *Petro Ranger*. According to the information given by the pirates to the captain of the *Petro Ranger*, Ken Blyth, the two smaller tankers had previously been hijacked by the same syndicate. The pirate leader, an Indonesian called Herman, claimed that his group operated under the protection of some senior Chinese naval officers and that there were Chinese naval personnel aboard the two smaller tankers. The diesel seems to have been destined for Hainan, where there was a thriving black market for fuel due to restrictions on the sale of fuel through legal distribution channels. Two pirates left the *Petro Ranger* aboard one of the smaller tankers to collect the payment for the cargo in cash.

After the discharge of the diesel, the *Petro Ranger* waited in the area for one of the smaller tankers to return with the money and unload the rest of the cargo. Eventually, four days later, another smaller tanker returned with the two pirates and the money. As the oil was being pumped over into the smaller vessel, however, they were intercepted by a Chinese marine police boat. The police took control over the two vessels and ordered them to go to the outer harbour of the port of Haikou in Hainan. Initially, the *Wilby* seems to have been suspected, not of piracy, but of smuggling, and the pirates, who, along with the original crew were allowed to stay on board, apparently believed that they would be released after investigations and possibly paying some bribes. The marine police authorities, however, seemed to suspect that the *Wilby* might in fact be the *Petro Ranger*, the disappearance of which had attracted widespread attention both in the media and by law enforcement authorities in the region. On 30 April, 14 days after the hijacking, the pirates were arrested and taken into custody in Haikou.

In contrast to the *Anna Sierra*, the *Petro Ranger* was returned to her owner by the Chinese authorities at the end of May. The authorities, however, kept the rest of the cargo and the money which the pirates had received for the sale of the diesel oil as 'evidence'. In spite of this, none of the pirates was prosecuted but were instead deported to Indonesia in mid-October and then apparently released.[21]

Even though the Chinese authorities were criticised for not prosecuting the pirates, their deportation to Indonesia may very well have been instrumental in the unravelling of part of the syndicate responsible for the hijacking of the *Petro Ranger* and at least four other commercial vessels in Southeast Asian waters. In late November and early December 1998, the Indonesian navy in Riau arrested a group of alleged syndicate members led by Chew Cheng Kiat, alias Mr Wong, a 56-year-old Singaporean who confessed to having staged five hijackings during the previous two years. Mr Wong operated from a small tanker, the *Pulau Mas*, which most of the time stayed in international waters. The items seized by the Indonesian authorities on board the *Pulau Mas* read as a list of the modern organised pirate's essential equipment kit – perhaps with the exception of firearms, none of which were reported to have been found on the *Pulau Mas*:[22]

- 15 pairs of handcuffs
- 14 ninja-style face masks
- three bayonets
- one speedboat powered by a 200-horsepower outboard engine and capable of doing 35 knots
- one Indonesian immigration stamp
- one date/time stamp
- false ship documents for five different vessel names
- eight templates for different ship names
- 12 cartons of paint of various colours
- a number of ship flags

The hijackings of Mr Wong's syndicate were carefully planned. The targets were chosen weeks before and false documentation prepared well ahead of the operation. The syndicate also had access to information about the ship's cargo and routes, and they generally employed a crew member from the target ship as an informant. Sometimes the hijacked ships were abandoned after the cargo had been discharged, whereas in other cases the ship was provided with a phantom identity and used for other purposes.[23] In all instances, the cargo was sold to China, where, as we have seen in the case of the *Petro Ranger*, the syndicate seemed to have established contacts with corrupt naval officials.

The reasons for the syndicates to hijack a ship obviously varied. In some cases, such as the *Petro Ranger*, the cargo was the main interest but in many other cases hijackings appear to have served an auxiliary function for more lucrative illicit activities, such as drug trafficking and human smuggling.[24] For example, the 700-ton cargo ship *Fu Tai*, which was hijacked off Batam in August 1998 – possibly by Mr Wong's syndicate – was reportedly provided with a phantom identity and used by drug smugglers to transport heroin between Thailand, the Philippines and Hong Kong.[25]

Human smuggling seems to have been a central factor in the demand for phantom vessels in the 1990s, and the surge in human smuggling roughly coincided with the surge in hijackings of vessels in East and Southeast Asia. The trade in illegal migrants from China to developed countries, particularly the United States, increased dramatically in the 1980s and early 1990s. In 1992 alone, an estimated 100,000 Chinese citizens, mostly from the province of Fujian in eastern China, entered the United States illegally. Organised syndicates of human smugglers, known as 'snakeheads', arranged for the migrants to enter the country in one of several ways, including overland from Canada or Mexico, by air or by sea. In 1993, a Western diplomat estimated that there were between 17 and 20 refitted cargo ships that crossed the Pacific Ocean between China and the United States, each with a capacity to carry hundreds of illegal migrants. The *Golden Venture*, which in June 1993 ran aground outside New York City with close to 300 illegal Chinese migrants on board, was one such vessel. This was operated by one of the major Chinese syndicates, the so-called Fuk Ching (Fujian) Gang. According to John Burnett, the small freighter had plied coastal routes in Southeast Asia before she was hijacked and renamed the *Golden Venture*.[26]

Earlier the same year, in February 1993, another human smuggling vessel, the *East Wood*, a 95-metre Panamanian-registered freighter, was boarded by United States Coastguards after having sent out a distress signal, some 2,400 kilometres southwest of Hawaii. On board were 525 Chinese men and women, each of whom had paid around US$ 30,000 to be smuggled into the United States.[27] According to press reports, the *East Wood* had been detained six months earlier by Public Security Bureau officials from Shekou in southern China as it was sailing along the Chinese coast with a cargo of cars bound for Vietnam. Charging that the cars might be smuggled into China overland after reaching Vietnam, the Chinese authorities seized the ship and its cargo worth US$ 7.5 million.[28]

In comparison, based on the number of illegal immigrants on board the *East Wood* and the fees charged by the snakeheads, the income from one load of illegal immigrants was around twice the value of *East Wood*'s original cargo of cars. Moreover, whereas the proceeds from selling the cargo of a hijacked commercial vessel was a one-time revenue, the proceeds from smuggling humans could be repeated several times over – possibly changing the name and identity of the vessel after each trip. Already in 1992, a United States Senate committee report estimated that the human smuggling business from China turned over US$ 3 billion per year – several times more than the combined economic losses incurred by all hijackings of commercial vessels in East and Southeast Asia during the 1990s.[29]

In the mid-1990s, virtually all major organised piracies in East and Southeast Asian waters seemed, in one way or another, to involve Chinese officials. In some cases, there were strong indications that Chinese law enforcement officials actually perpetrated pirate attacks in Chinese as well as international waters. In other cases, hijacked ships turned up in Chinese ports, where officials either sold the cargo or tried to extort money from the owners of the vessel. The organised syndicates that were responsible for most hijackings obviously colluded with corrupt Chinese officials to sell their stolen cargoes and vessels and to protect them from arrest and prosecution. In 1998, these circumstances led the IMB and the Baltic and International Maritime Council (BIMCO) to make an official protest on behalf of the maritime industry to the Chinese government.[30] At the 71st session of the Maritime Safety Committee of the IMO the following year, moreover, the Chinese delegation was forced to defend itself against allegations that China did not do enough to combat piracy.[31]

The international pressure contributed to prompt the Chinese government to take measures against the corruption in the maritime sphere but, even more importantly, the widespread corruption had developed into a serious economic problem for the government itself. From mid-1998, the concept of 'economic security' was launched by China's top leaders as a key national goal and, apart from illegal financial transfers, smuggling was the issue of the greatest concern. The involvement of the military in oil smuggling was seen as particularly problematic, as this activity had begun to distort prices and create serious economic difficulties for the country's two oil monopolies. In July, a national conference on how to crack down on smuggling was convened in Beijing. At the conference, China's President Jiang Zemin declared that smuggling activities had reached unprecedented levels and posed a serious threat to the economy, and Prime Minister Zhu Rongji, expressing his concern over the involvement in smuggling by party and government officials, estimated that some 100 billion Yuan (US$ 12 billion) worth of commodities were smuggled into China each year. The conference resulted in the establishment of a new Anti-smuggling Criminal Investigation Bureau controlled directly by the central government and in command of a special anti-smuggling police unit. At the same time, the government also took several steps to tighten China's borders, and numerous corrupt officials were discharged. In Guangdong, Zhu Rongji personally oversaw the firing of 600 allegedly corrupt officials in October 1998.[32]

The Chinese crackdown on corruption not only deprived the organised pirate syndicates of their main market for hijacked vessels and stolen cargoes; it also signalled the end of impunity for the perpetrators of pirate attacks in the country. In November 1998, the *Cheung Son*, a 10,000-ton bulk carrier carrying a load of furnace slag bound for Malaysia, was hijacked in the Taiwan Strait by a group of pirates posing as Chinese customs and security officials. After being held hostage for 10 days, all 23 crew members were rounded up on deck and clubbed, shot or stabbed do death. Their corpses – six of which were later caught in the nets of Chinese fishermen – were weighted down with metal engine parts and thrown overboard. Subsequent police investigations in China led to the arrest of more than 50 alleged pirates, some of whom had also been involved in several previous attacks. In December 1999, a court in Shanwei found 38 of the alleged pirates guilty of the *Cheung Son* hijacking, 13 of whom were sentenced to death and executed in January 2000.[33]

In spite of the investigations and harsh sentences, however, the reason behind the hijacking of the *Cheung Son* remains a mystery and those ultimately responsible for the hijacking are probably still free. The cargo of furnace slag was nearly worthless, and the 21-year-old vessel itself was of little value. After being hijacked and provided with a phantom identity, the *Cheung Son* was reportedly sold, first within China for US$ 36,000, and then to an unknown Singaporean buyer for US$ 300,000[34] – a relatively small amount in comparison to the average 'haul' of around US$ 1–2 million for a hijacking. According to international authorities, cited by *The Economist*, the *Cheung Son* may have been used for illegal export of Chinese arms.[35] The Intermediate People's Court in Shanwei, however, established that the hijacking and killings had been ordered by a local businessman, Weng Siliang, who was one of the 13 men sentenced to death by the court and executed. Meanwhile, the operational leader of the hijacking, an Indonesian named Wei Suoni, alias Sony Wei, told the court that the hijacking had been ordered by Liem Sioe Liong, a Chinese Indonesian tycoon who had close relations with Indonesia's former President Suharto and who up until the 1997–1998 economic crisis was the country's richest man.[36] The allegations against Liem seem not to have been investigated any further, neither by the Chinese nor the Indonesian authorities, but fuelled suspicions – still unsubstantiated – that the Fujianese Liem might have been linked to the Fuk Ching syndicate and involved in various transnational criminal activities, such as piracy, human smuggling and trafficking.[37]

The stiff sentences against the *Cheung Son* hijackers, coupled with the Chinese government's firm resolution to crack down on smuggling and corruption, obviously had a considerable deterring effect on the organised pirate gangs. According to Noel Choong, regional director of the IMB's Piracy Reporting Centre, the result has been that hijackers since around 2000 have tended to avoid China.[38] The crackdown on piracy and corruption in China, moreover, seems to have been sustained, and in January 2003 the hijackers of a Thai oil tanker, *Siam Xanxai*, in June 1999 were sentenced to between 10 and 15 years in prison. These stiff punishments for the members of organised pirate gangs in China were also paralleled in other Asian countries, including Indonesia where Mr Wong, in August 1999, was sentenced to six years in prison for ordering piratical raids.[39] In India, meanwhile, a Mumbai court in February 2003 sentenced 14 of the pirates responsible for the hijacking of a chemical tanker, *Alondra Rainbow*, in October 1999 to seven years of 'rigorous imprisonment', that is, hard labour.[40] The arrests and stiff sentences of dozens of members of organised pirate gangs probably contributed strongly to a substantial decline in the number of hijackings from 1999, as did the increasing success of the IMB in assisting the law enforcement authorities in recovering hijacked vessels.

International efforts to enhance maritime security in the wake of attacks against the World Trade Centre in New York on 11 September 2001 have also made it considerably more difficult for pirates to succeed in hijacking commercial vessels. Since 2004 all international trading vessels over 500 gross tonnes are required to be equipped with an Automatic Identification Systems (AIS) that via satellite communicate information about the ship's identity, position, heading and speed to other AIS-equipped ships and to shore-based, government-operated facilities. This means that, in most cases, a hijacked ship can easily be located by law enforcement authorities anywhere in the world.[41] This regulation makes it much more difficult for pirates to provide a hijacked ship with a phantom identity.

As a consequence of these developments, the syndicates seem more or less to have abandoned the hijackings of commercial vessels, and there were no major hijackings involving the long-term seizure of a commercial vessel in Southeast Asia between October 2002 and late September 2005.[42] On 30 September 2005, however, the 59-metre long Indonesian general cargo vessel *Prima Indah* was hijacked by pirates armed with automatic rifles and knives three hours after leaving Bangka in South Sumatra for Singapore with a cargo of 660 tons of tin ingots worth around US$ 4.7 million. The 14 crew members were released and rescued by some passing fishing boats.[43]

As hijackings of commercial vessels declined sharply in Southeast Asia in the first years of the twenty-first century, however, hijackings of tugs and barges increased instead, possibly because some of those responsible for hijackings of commercial vessels in the 1990s shifted to the softer targets which tugs and barges comprise. Even though normally such vessels are of little value in themselves, they often carry valuable cargoes of several thousand tonnes of easily disposable bulk commodities, particularly valuable palm oil which seems to be the preferred cargo of the hijackers. Tugs and barges are also slow and easy to board and, being relatively small and not drawing much water, they are easy to hide. Most of them look alike, which means that they can be easily repainted and provided with a phantom identity and either sold or used for illegal activities such as smuggling and cargo fraud. All hijacked tugs have also been smaller than 500 gross tonnes and thus not subject to the new security measures adopted by the IMO in 2002, such as the requirement to install the AIS and to prominently and permanently display their identification numbers.

Between September 2001 and September 2005 there were 22 reported hijackings of tugs and barges in Southeast Asia. Mainly the incidents were concentrated to the southern Malacca Strait region, where 17 of the reported incidents occurred. In addition, there were three hijackings in other parts of Southeast Asia, one in the South China Sea, one off the South Sumatra coast and one in the Sulu Sea. Two cases in which tugs and barges disappeared with their entire crews were also reported from around the Makassar Strait. According to witness reports, the hijackers were generally armed with guns and/or knives, but serious violence seems, in most cases, to have been avoided and there were no reports of shootings in the hijackings in 2002 or 2003. This, however, does not necessarily mean that there were no casualties.In some cases, the crew jumped, or were forced to jump, overboard and swam for the shore. In at least one such incident, a crew member drowned after being forced to jump overboard, and in another incident nine out of ten crew members who were forced off their ship at sea went missing and presumably drowned. Altogether, dozens of crew members are to date missing as a result of the attacks on tugs and barges since 2001, most of whom probably were killed by the pirates or drowned after being forced off their vessel.[44]

The hijackings of tugs and barges are obviously organised in that they require a relatively high degree of planning beforehand in order to escape with the hijacked vessel and dispose of the vessel and cargo. The nationality of the perpetrators, their *modus operandi* and the geographic distribution of the attacks, however, all indicate that they are the work of the opportunistic pirate gangs that were described in the previous chapter. This apparent contradiction can be explained by several indications that the organised syndicates recently have started to contract whole gangs of local pirates in Indonesia's Riau archipelago to carry out the hijackings. According to Husni, a Riau pirate leader cited by the Indonesian magazine *Latitudes* in October 2003:

> These days we work on a contractual basis. All we have to do is wait for an order to come in, with the coordinates of where the ship is to be attacked. Our forces go in, take the ship and capture the sailors. Then the replacement crew (a group of professional sailors) comes in to deliver the ship to the customer.[45]

This 'outsourcing' of piratical activity makes sense, both from the point of view of the petty pirates in the southern Malacca Strait and the organised syndicates. A few years earlier, still according to *Latitudes*, Husni had worried about declining returns from piracy because of the expansion of electronic money transfers which meant that commercial vessels tended to carry less cash than before. Working for organised syndicates, by contrast, had meant that his income had risen substantially. For the syndicates, an obvious advantage of the arrangement is that the pirates need only to have a minimum of contact with, and knowledge about, the organisation that orders the hijacking. The replacement crew that takes over from the pirates and sail the vessel to its destination, moreover, has no information about the actual hijacking and, if arrested, they will not be recognised by the original crew or in any other way implicated in the attack.

The consequence is that the distinction between opportunistic piratical activity and organised maritime criminal activities, including hijackings, has become more blurred in recent years. The executions and heavy prison sentences handed out to several of the perpetrators of organised pirate attacks in China, India and Indonesia in the late 1990s and early 2000s probably contributed to a substantial decline in the number of hijackings of commercial vessels in Southeast Asia after the surge in the late 1980s and 1990s. The verdicts, however, did not put an end to the activities of the organised syndicates in the region. Instead, their targets shifted, primarily to tugs and barges which are more easily attacked and disguised than commercial vessels but the cargoes of which may be at least as valuable. Also, along with the shift from commercial vessels to tugs and barges, a new form of organisation seems to have emerged in which the syndicates have started to contract gangs of local petty pirates (mainly, it seems, from Indonesia's Riau archipelago) to carry out the hijackings for them. Against this background, it seems that the opportunistic pirate gangs that since the early 1980s have worked more or less independently in the Singapore Strait and southern parts of the Malacca Strait are currently in the process of being drawn closer into the activities of some of the larger organised transnational crime syndicates operating in the region.

Notes

1 ICC – International Maritime Bureau (1994b: 9).

2 Abhyankar (2001: 179).

3 The following summary is mainly based on ibid.

4 *Far Eastern Economic Review* (16 November 1979).

5 Ibid.

6 'Report of the IMO Working Group on the Malacca Strait Area', IMO MCS 62/INF.3 (1993), p. 16; see also Abhyankar (2001: 168) about the background to the formation of the IMB. Piracy, however, was not a major priority of the IMB at the time of its founding. Only two years later, in 1983, did the IMO call on the Bureau to report on the current situation concerning armed attacks against ships, a request that was repeated in 1984 and 1985, resulting in three reports to the IMO on the problem of piracy and armed robbery from merchant ships; see Hyslop (1989: 3). The IMB's Regional Piracy Centre, subsequently the Piracy Reporting Centre, was only set up in 1992; see further in Chapter 6.

7 Abhyankar (2001: 175).

8 See ibid. (2001: 158–162) and *Far Eastern Economic Review* (16 February 1984).

9 Ellen (1992: 20).

10 ICC – International Maritime Bureau (1994b: 9–10).

11 ICC – International Maritime Bureau (1992a: 7).

12 *New Straits Times* (15 December 1992). John Burnett (2002: 134–143) has also argued that organised pirates may have been involved in the collision between the *Ocean Blessing* and the *Nagasaki Spirit* in the Malacca Strait on 19 September 1992.

13 The vessels were *MV* [Motor vessel] *Jui Ho* (1994), *MV Alicia Star* (1994), *MV Tequila* (1994), *MV Anna Sierra* (1995), *MV Hye Mieko* (1995), *MT* [Motor tanker] *Suci* (1996), *MT Lung Shun No. 8* (1997), *MV Vosa Carrier* (1997) and *MT Atlanta 95* (1997); see ICC – International Maritime Bureau (1995: 5–6, 1996: 4–5, 1997: 4–5, 1998a: 14, 15, 22).

14 The narrative is condensed from ICC – International Maritime Bureau (1998b: 40–46).

15 Renwick and Abbott (1999: 186–187) and Chalk (1998: 93–94); see also ibid. (2000: 70).

16 ICC – International Maritime Bureau (1996: 5).

17 Chalk (2000: 180, n. 19, 60–61); italics in original.

18 Interview with Noel Choong, regional director of the IMB Piracy Reporting Centre, Kuala Lumpur, 16 January 2004. See also Abhyankar (2001: 181).

19 ICC – International Maritime Bureau (1994b: 11).

20 The following account of the hijacking of the *Petro Ranger* is based on a critical reading of the book later published by the master of vessel, Captain Ken Blyth (2000). A point of controversy (not further raised here) concerns whether or not Blyth had ordered that basic precautions against piracy be taken before the hijacking; see Burnett (2002: 228).

21 According to Blyth (2000: 30), seven of the pirates were Indonesians, three were Malaysians and two were Thai. All of them, however, carried forged Indonesian passports. John Burnett (2002: 229–232) later interviewed one of them, Darman Djuki, who was still a free man several years after the hijacking of the *Petro Ranger.*

22 *Sijori Pos* (8 and 9 December 1998).

23 Ibid.

24 Abhyankar (2001: 181).

25 Burnett (2002: 222–223). In contrast to Burnett's report that the *Fu Tai* was a 'new whip with nice lines, clean grey hull, and yellow funnel', however, newspaper reports described the ship as old and dilapidated. This circumstance, paired with the owner's apparent unwillingness to help tracing the ship, arouses suspicions that the ship's disappearance might be related to attempted insurance fraud; see *Sijori Pos* (15 and 19 August 1998).

26 Burnett (2002: 220).

27 *Far Eastern Economic Review* (8 April 1993).

28 *Wall Street Journal* (Eastern edition), 2 June 1993.

29 See *Far Eastern Economic Review* (8 April 1993). More recently, the number of Chinese smuggled into the United States appears to have declined somewhat. According to an International Crime Threat Assessment prepared in 2000 by an interagency working group of the United States government, between 30,000 and 40,000 Chinese were smuggled into the country in 1999. The fee, however, seemed to have risen to an average of US$ 60,000, according to Ko-Lin Chin, professor of criminal justice at Rutgers University; cited by *Forbes* (7 June 2004). With 25,000 people being smuggled by boat to the United States from China's Fujian province each year, this section of the illegal migration industry would still have a turn-over of around US$ 1.5 billion.

30 ICC – International Maritime Bureau (1999: 17).

31 'Report of the Maritime Safety Committee on its seventy-first session', IMO MSC 71/23/15.4 (2 June 1999).

32 Fewsmith (1999: 105–107).

33 Liss (2003: 52–53) and Burnett (2002: 224–225). See also Lintner (2003: 1–2) for a vivid description of the atmosphere surrounding the execution.

34 Liss (2003: 52).

35 *The Economist* (18 December 1999).

36 Liss (2003: 53).

37 See the 1999 Penguin Star article 'Piracy Returns as Order in the High Seas Disappears', at the Internet web page http://www.geocities.com/Yosemite/7915/9901/Pirates.html, accessed on 20 November 2003. Also indicating the involvement of Liem – but without mentioning his name – was *The Economist*'s (19 December 1999) observation that one of the organised pirate syndicates 'is thought to be headed by an Indonesian tycoon who was one of former President Suharto's closest business pals'. Similar allegations involving Liem have been raised by Frécon (2002: 74) and van de Bunt and Pladdet (2003: 41).

38 Interview by the author, Kuala Lumpur, 16 January 2004.

39 *Sijori Pos* (27 August 1999).

40 ICC News Archives, 25 February 2003, available at the Internet web page http://www.iccwbo.org/home/news_archives/2003/stories/alondra.asp, accessed on 23 September 2005.

41 The regulations are part of a package, involving changes to the Safety of Life at Sea (SOLAS) Convention and the introduction of a new International Ship and Port Facility Security (ISPS) Code, adopted by the Maritime Safety Committee of the IMO at its 76th session in December 2002. The regulations also require vessels to 'prominently and permanently' display their unique identification number, meaning that it must by embossed, punched or cut into the ship, something which also will facilitate the identification and recovery of hijacked vessels. See Organization for Economic Co-operation and Development (2003: 30–40) for a summary of the adopted security measures.

42 On 28 September 2002, the Malaysian oil tanker *Nautica Kluang* was hijacked and its cargo of diesel oil was transferred to another ship and stolen; see ICC – International Maritime Bureau (2003: 20). The only reported hijacking in Southeast Asia in 2003–2004 occurred on 10 August 2003 when another Malaysian tanker, *Penrider*, was hijacked in the Malacca Strait; see ICC – International Maritime Bureau (2004:

20). The pirates, however, seemed to take no interest in the ship or its cargo, and she was released seven hours after the she was attacked. Leaving the ship, the pirates kidnapped the master, chief engineer and greaser and held them for ransom. The target and *modus operandi* indicate that the perpetrators were members of one of the Acehnese groups which since 2001 have conducted kidnappings for ransom in the northern Malacca Strait rather than of an international organised criminal group.

On 22 April 2005, the Indonesian general cargo ship *Inabukwa* was also hijacked off Lingga island in Riau. The pirates discharged the ship's cargo but then released the vessel and the crew; see ICC – International Maritime Bureau (2005b: 17).

43 Sydney Morning Herald (Internet edition) (4 October 2005), available at the Internet web page http://smh.com.au/news/world/pirates-hijack-ship-with-6m-cargo/2005/10/04/1128191697099.html, accessed on 5 October 2005. At the time of writing, the vessel and its cargo are still missing.

44 For the incidents, see ICC – International Maritime Bureau (2002, 2003, 2004, 2005a and 2005b).

45 *Latitudes*, vol. 33 (October 2003). The article does not specifically say that Husni and his pirate gang were responsible for the spate of hijackings of tugs and barges in the area. However, as there were no reported hijackings of commercial vessels in the area in 2003, and only one in 2002, it seems likely that the attacks referred to involved tugs and barges. The type of arrangement, moreover, seems to have been in place for some years; see the story in Time (Asian Internet edition) (20 August 2001). See also *Far Eastern Economic Review* (27 May 2004) about the links between organised criminals and local petty pirates based in Indonesia.

CHAPTER 6

The Counts and Costs of Piracy

PIRACY, THROUGHOUT THIS BOOK, is understood in the broad popular sense of the word as such acts of robbery or violence upon the sea that, if committed on land, would amount to felony.[1] The scope of this book also covers coastal raiding because the two activities are closely related and often perpetrated by the same individuals. This vernacular understanding of the concept of 'piracy', however, differs from the definition of the word in international law, as well as from the other main definition in use today, the one established and employed by the International Maritime Bureau. The purpose here is not to dwell on legal technicalities and problems in the definition of piracy but rather to discuss how statistical information on piracy is influenced by interpretations of what is considered to be piracy and by how piracy is reported. This information, in turn, is central in forming much of the public impressions about the scope and character of piratical activity around the world over the past decades.[2]

In international law, piracy is defined by article 101 of the 1982 United Nations Convention on the Law of the Sea (UNCLOS). According to that article, piracy consists of the following acts:

(a) any illegal acts of violence or detention, or any act of depreda-tion, committed for private ends by the crew or the pas-sengers of a private ship or a private aircraft, and directed:
   (i) on the high seas, against another ship or aircraft, or against persons or property on board such ship or aircraft;
   (ii) against a ship, aircraft, persons or property in a place outside the jurisdiction of any State;

(b) any act of voluntary participation in the operation of a ship or of an aircraft with knowledge of facts making it a pirate ship or aircraft;

(c) any act of inciting or of intentionally facilitating an act described in subparagraph (a) or (b).

The UNCLOS definition thus stipulates that piracy, by definition, occurs on the high seas, that is, outside the jurisdiction of any state. Moreover, it presumes that two ships – that is, a pirate ship and a target ship – are involved, thus excluding coastal raids and attacks on vessels at berth from land. The provision that piracy must be committed for 'private ends' also, in principle, excludes illegal acts perpetrated by the vessels of any government on the high seas.

The UNCLOS definition should not be taken to mean that piratical activity only occurs on the high seas – in fact most reported attacks (over 70 per cent in 2004)[3] take place in territorial waters. As a piece of international law, however, UNCLOS only regulates issues that concern the high seas or the maritime relations between states since anything else would mean an infringement on the sovereignty of the nation states that are signatories to the Convention. Consequently, piracy may also be defined and regulated in various national legislations. In order to avoid confusion, however, the concept 'armed robbery against ships' has, at least since the 1980s, been used by the International Maritime Organization to describe such piratical acts (as defined by article 101 in UNCLOS) that take place within a State's jurisdiction over such offences.

The other major current definition of piracy has been formulated by the International Maritime Bureau and takes the perspective of the main victims of the attacks, that is, the crews and owners of the attacked vessels and their cargo. Until recently, the IMB did not distinguish between 'piracy' and 'armed robbery against ships', only defining piracy as 'an act of boarding or attempting to board any ship with the apparent intent to commit theft or any other crime and with the apparent intent or capability to use force in the furtherance of that act', regardless of whether the crime took place on the high seas or within the jurisdiction of a state. In 2001, however, the

Bureau altered its definition in harmony with the concepts used by the IMO, thus distinguishing between piracy that takes place on the high seas and armed robbery against ships that takes place in territorial waters.[4] At the same time, the 22nd Assembly of the IMO adopted a Code of Practice for the Investigation of Crimes of Piracy and Armed Robbery against Ships, which stated:

> Armed Robbery against Ships means any unlawful act of violence or detention or any act of depredation, or threat thereof, other than an act of 'piracy', directed against a ship or against persons or property on board such ship, within a State's jurisdiction over such offences.[5]

Most importantly, both the IMO and the IMB definitions of 'piracy and armed robbery against ships' now cover all attacks – attempted as well as actual – against ships regardless of whether they occur in port (at anchor or berth), in territorial waters or on the high seas. The rationale behind the definitions is, as put by the IMB, that the differentiation between piracy and armed robbery has no relevance for the crew of ships under attack.[6] Statistically, however, the adoption of these definitions, combined with a gradually increasing share of incidents that are reported, has meant that the number of pirate and armed robbery attacks against ships has increased since the 1980s.

The problem of piracy was first brought up on the agenda of the IMO – or, more precisely, the Maritime Safety Committee of the IMO – by the government of Sweden, which in 1983 submitted a note on the increasing incidence of piracy targeting international shipping in 'certain coastal areas of the world'.[7] The Swedish government was particularly concerned over several violent attacks against merchant vessels off West Africa, but also mentioned the Singapore Strait (along with the Bay of Suez) as an area where several piratical incidents had occurred in the recent past. The note – which was supported by a concerned plea by several shipping organisations, including the Baltic and International Maritime Conference (BIMCO) and the International Shipping Federation, and trade unions, for the IMO to take measures to improve the situation – led to the drafting of a resolution, adopted by the IMO in November the same year, on 'Measures to Prevent Acts of Piracy and Armed Robbery against Ships'.[8] The resolution urged governments to 'take, as a matter of the highest priority, all measures necessary to prevent and suppress acts of piracy and armed robbery against ships in or adjacent to their waters, including strengthening of security measures'. It also requested that governments inform the IMO of 'any act of piracy or armed robbery committed against a ship flying the flag of their country, indicating the location and circumstances of the incident and the action taken by the coastal state'.

The resolution meant that piracy went from having been considered by the international maritime community principally as a long-since extinct threat to shipping to being a major contemporary security concern. From 1984 onwards, piracy and armed robbery against ships has been a standing item on the agenda of annual sessions of the Maritime Safety Committee of the IMO, and in the same year the organisation started, in accordance with the resolution, to collect information about piratical attacks from flag states and to summarise the information in the form of lists of attacks circulated among the organisation's member states.

The information which the IMO received, however, only reflected a fraction of the all attacks that actually took place. Throughout the 1980s, most of the information came from a handful of flag states – notably West Germany, Greece and Japan – that appeared to take the request to report incidents the organisation seriously, whereas most member states did not submit any information at all. Even Sweden, which had taken the initiative with the resolution, only reported one case of an attack against a Swedish-flagged vessel in the 1980s, although it seems likely that several more attacks against vessels under the country's flag did occur.[9]

There were several reasons why flag states did not report incidents to the IMO. Even if shipowners reported an attack to the flag state (rather than to the coastal or port states where the attack took place) it is not certain that, because of administrative inefficiency, such an attack was reported to the relevant authority submitting information to the IMO. As regards domestic armed robberies against ships – that is, when the ship of a certain flag state was attacked in the waters of that same state – this is likely to have been seen as a domestic police matter and not reported to the IMO especially since such incidents were likely to be seen as harmful to that country's international reputation.

There were also several reasons for shipowners not to report attacks against their vessels, neither to the flag or coastal state. A 1983 report by the International Maritime Bureau to the IMO on the problem of piracy and armed robbery from merchant ships identified four reasons for not reporting pirate attacks: (1) the potential for bad publicity, especially if incidents are reported to the press and sensationalised; (2) the danger of local, unofficial discrimination if a shipowner complains of the security in a particular port area; (3) possible problems with crew unions if the danger in certain areas is deemed unacceptable; and (4) the risk of rising insurance premiums.[10] To these, a fifth major reason can be added, namely the risk that an attacked vessel might be delayed for several days for investigations, something which easily could prove more costly for the shipping company than the incurred loss from an attack.

As a consequence, the figures provided by the IMO in the 1980s probably only reflected a minority of the number of attacks actually taking place. In spite of the under-reporting, however, the figures can be compared over time and probably say something about how piracy fluctuated in different parts of the world. After a peak of more than 100 reported incidents worldwide in 1985, the situation improved and stabilised – providing for statistical variation – at around half of that number in the period from 1986 to 1989. The decline in the total incidence of piracy and armed robbery in the world was mainly due to improvements in the situation in the waters off West Africa after 1985. In the Straits of Malacca and Singapore, meanwhile, the number of reported incidents was relatively constant after the first wave of piracy in the area between 1981 and 1983 had been suppressed, and from the mid-1980s to 1990, there were on average around 20 reported attacks each year. In addition, a handful of attacks were reported in the South China Sea each year, increasing somewhat toward the end of the decade.[11]

From around 1990, however, the number of reported attacks in the Malacca Strait region and the South China Sea increased dramatically, resulting in a tripling of the total number of attacks worldwide between 1989 and 1992 from around 50 to more than 150. Several member states, as well as the International Shipping Federation, expressed concern over the increase in the number of incidents, and in 1992, the Maritime Safety Committee, at its 60th session, reiterated its request that member states report all attacks to the IMO.[12] Moreover, the failure of member states to report to the IMO was demonstrated as the observer of the IMB at the session provided information about attacks in 1991 which far exceeded the number of attacks reported to the IMO. The IMB listed 107 attacks in 1991 in Far Eastern waters, whereas the IMO only had received reports of 33 attacks – over half of which were reported by Japan. Apart from Japan, only six member states – Denmark, India, the Netherlands, Norway, South Korea and Switzerland – submitted reports of attacks in 1991 to the IMO ahead of the Committee's session.[13]

Against the background of a sharply increasing number of piratical attacks from the early 1990s, especially in East and Southeast Asian waters, and in view of the apparent failure of the authorities of flag states to report incidents to the IMO, representatives of the shipping industry decided to set up a non-government anti-piracy centre in Kuala Lumpur. The centre was to be operated by the IMB and financed through voluntary contributions – initially US$ 200,000 – from the industry.[14] Before the centre began operating, however, the initiative was condemned by officials in the region, who apparently feared that its activities would cause a further deterioration of the region's already tarnished international reputation as a pirate-infested area. Indonesia's director of naval operations and training, Commodore Sutedjo, was especially outspoken in his criticism and, speaking at the first major international conference on Southeast Asian piracy in Kuala Lumpur in July 1992, he said that the number of piracies in the region was small and that the coastal states in the region were able to handle them successfully. He thus rejected the idea of an international anti-piracy centre, saying that it would be 'wasting and uneffective' [sic].[15]

In spite of the opposition, the IMB established the Regional Piracy Centre in Kuala Lumpur in October 1992. The name and location of the Centre seemed to indicate that it was primarily to be concerned with piracy in East and Southeast Asia, but it was in fact from the beginning concerned with piratical activities also in other parts of the world, and in 1997, the name was changed to the more apt Piracy Reporting Centre. Today, the Centre provides five main services:[16]

- To receive reports of suspicious or unexplained craft movements, boarding and armed robbery from ships and to alert other ships and law enforcement agencies in the area;
- To issue regular status reports of piracy and armed robbery via daily broadcasts on Inmarsat-C through its SafetyNET service;[17]
- To collate and analyse information received and issue consolidated reports to relevant bodies, including the International Maritime Organization;
- To assist owners and crews of ships that have been attacked;
- To locate vessels that have been seized by pirates and recover stolen cargoes.

The work of the Piracy Reporting Centre has meant that a much greater share of pirate attacks are reported today than in the 1980s and early 1990s when the main responsibility for the reporting fell on the flag states. In the course of the 1990s, the Centre also became increasingly well known among shipmasters and owners, probably further increasing the percentage of attacks that were reported.[18] Even so, the IMB estimates that only about half of the actual number of attacks is reported, mainly because of the reluctance on the part of shipowners to report attacks against their vessels.[19]

Today, as for most of the previous decade, the IMB is the main source of information and figures about contemporary piracy. Its annual reports, normally published at the end of each January for the previous year, are widely cited in the media and form the basis of many, if not most, analyses of the problem. Even the IMO has come to rely almost exclusively on the information provided by the IMB for its piracy reports. In 2004, all but five of the 330 incidents of piracy and armed robbery against ships reported to the IMO and published in its annual report were reported to the organisation by the IMB. Only three of the IMO's 165 member states – Colombia, Liberia and the United Arab Emirates – reported attacks occurring in 2004 to the IMO.[20] It thus seems that the services provided by the IMB have led most flag states to consider their reporting to the IMO to be superfluous.

In spite of the considerable improvements in the reporting of incidents of piracy and armed robbery against ships due to the efforts of the Piracy Reporting Centre, its statistics have also been the subject of criticism, not least from government officials and analysts based in Southeast Asia. The IMB claims that petty thefts are excluded in their reporting of incidents of piracy and armed robbery unless the thieves are armed. But, from the narrations provided, several of the cases listed by the IMB as armed robberies or attempted armed robberies in port areas look to be little more than cases of petty theft or attempted petty theft, and there is often no information as to whether the thieves were armed or not. Consider, for example, the following condensed reports of so-called armed robberies in Southeast Asian ports, taken from the IMB's annual report for 2004:[21]

Vessel: *Tamarugal* (bulk carrier, 26,098 gross tons)
Date: 4 January 2004
Position: Balikpapan Outer Anchorage, Indonesia
Narration: While at anchor, five pirates boarded the ship via hawse pipe. They entered the bosun's store and stole ship's stores and safety equipment.

Vessel: *Stolt Hawk* (chemical tanker, 21,043 gross tons)
Date: 4 May 2004
Position: SPA Oil Berth, Sandakan Port, Malaysia
Narration: While at berth, the duty officer on routine rounds on board the tanker spotted three persons attempting

	to break the padlock of the forecastle store. He raised the alarm and the intruders jumped overboard and escaped empty-handed.
Vessel:	*Platres* (tanker, 54,962 gross tons)
Date:	26 October 2004
Position:	Dumai Anchorage, Indonesia
Narration:	While at anchor, three robbers boarded the tanker. Alert crew raised the alarm, activated fire hoses and the robbers fled.

These are scarcely incidents that normally – in the vernacular sense – would be understood as 'piracy', or even armed robbery. Nor is there conclusive evidence that these types of incident have increased in recent decades, even though there may have been geographic shifts in where in the world they are most prolific. In the 1960s, thefts from commercial vessels by local perpetrators posing as salesmen were, for example, common at both ends of the Suez Canal as ships waited at anchor to pass through the canal.[22] In those days, however, such incidents were not reported as acts of piracy, nor were they considered as such by the victims.

This should be borne in mind when considering figures in the IMB's annual piracy reports pointing to an alarming increase in recent years in the number of armed robberies against ships in Indonesian waters, most of them incidents in port areas (see Figure 1). This increase, however, does not solely (or maybe not even primarily) reflect a real rise in the number of attacks. For the most part, the increase is probably attributable to the improvements in the IMB's reporting and to the increasing acceptance among the members of the international shipping community of the Bureau's broad definition of piracy and armed robbery.

The IMB, as well as the IMO, sees the problem of piracy mainly from the point of view of the victims, i.e. the crews and ship-owners of the target ships, and from that perspective it makes sense to report all acts of violence or depredation against vessels whether they are at berth, anchor or underway. From the point of view of the

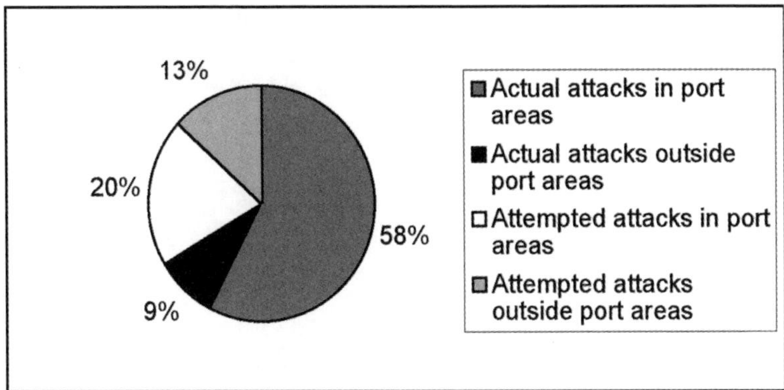

Figure 1: Actual and attempted attacks in Indonesian waters, 1995–2004
Source: ICC – International Maritime Bureau (1996–2005).

governments responsible for maintaining security in their waters and port areas, however, the reporting by the IMB of incidents of petty theft and attempted boardings in harbours may be seen as an irritant as they tend to give the impression that armed robberies against vessels underway are more common in their territorial and archipelagic waters than they actually are. For example, in 2004, the IMB reported 93 actual and attempted attacks in Indonesian waters – more than a quarter of all reported attacks worldwide. According to the IMO, however, eleven of these actually occurred in international waters. Of the remaining 82 attacks, 60 (or roughly three quarters) occurred in port areas, leaving only 22 attacks against vessels underway.[23] In all, the IMB reported 168 incidents in Southeast Asian waters (including the South China Sea and Vietnamese waters), out of which 76 occurred in ports, mainly in Indonesia. If these are separated from the attacks against steaming vessels, both in territorial waters and on the high seas, a rather different map of the distribution of piratical activity in the region emerges. What is left are 92 cases of actual and attempted attacks at sea (in addition to two cases of spotted suspicious craft), heavily concentrated to three adjacent regions along the east coast of Sumatra: the northern parts of the Malacca Strait (34 cases), the southern parts of the Malacca Strait

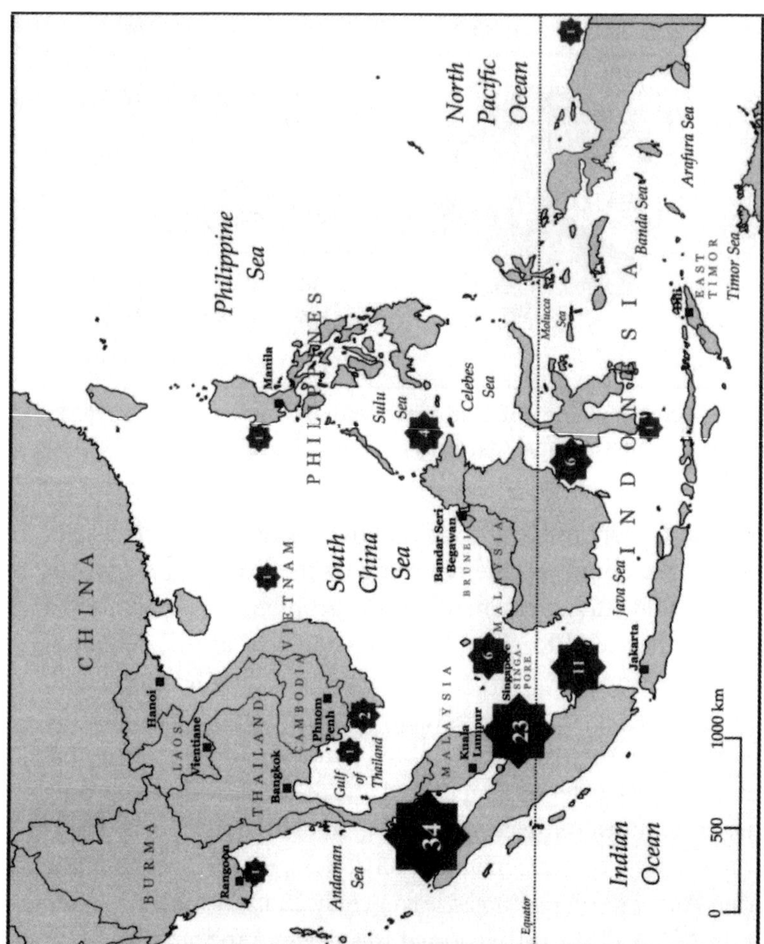

Map 6: Attacks against ships underway, 2004

including Singapore Strait and Indonesia's Riau-Lingga archipelago (23 cases), and the waters east of southern Sumatra (11 cases) (see Map 6). Together these areas accounted for close to 74 per cent of all reported attacks at sea in Southeast Asia. Other areas with several cases reported were the southwest parts of the South China Sea (6 cases), the Makassar Strait east of Indonesian Borneo (6 cases) and the Sulu region of the southern Philippines and eastern Sabah (4 cases). Even though the figures stand out as high in international comparison, they hardly justify descriptions of Southeast Asia or the Malacca Strait as a 'high risk' – that is, war zone – area, as recently declared by the Joint War Committee of Lloyd's of London. With around 200 ships transiting the Strait daily, the risk for an individual ship of being attacked was between 0.1 and 0.2 per cent in 2004.[24]

Whereas the human cost of piratical activity in the Strait of Malacca should not be made light of – particularly the violent kidnappings for ransom in the northern parts of the Strait and the hijackings of tugs and barges in its southern parts – the economic cost of piracy for the shipping industry as a whole is not very significant, even if attacks in port areas are included. According to Captain Jayant Abhyankar of the IMB, the average loss from a low-level armed robbery is around US$ 5,000 and from a hijacking between US$ 1 and 2 million.[25] Even in 2000, when the highest number of attacks in the Malacca Strait was recorded, the combined economic cost due to low-level armed robberies (75 reported cases) was only some US$ 750,000, if account is taken of the estimated under-reporting of half of the actual cases. The total value of the interregional maritime shipments passing through the Strait of Malacca, meanwhile, is well over US$ 500 billion, in relation to which the cost of piracy in the Strait is somewhere in the range of between 0.001 and 0.002 per cent.[26] The combined economic cost of hijackings is obviously much higher, although not very significant either in relation to the total value of maritime trade or the turnover of the global shipping industry. Indeed, currently, the problem has had little impact on international shipping, as most victims of hijackings in the region in recent years have been locally owned and managed tugs and barges.

For the littoral states, particularly Indonesia, the cost of effective patrolling of its vast territorial waters would be much higher than the losses incurred by piracy and armed robbery against the domestic shipping industry. For Indonesia, the economic relevance of the problem is, moreover, minimal when compared to the estimated cost of other illegal maritime activities, such as illegal fishing and maritime smuggling of various consumer goods and natural products, such as sand and timber. The figures are uncertain, but in 2003 the Indonesian government estimated that the country lost Rp 90 trillion (US$ 10 billion) because of illegal fishing, sand smuggling and illegal logging.[27] Poaching alone – mainly in the country's extensive 200-mile exclusive economic zone as regulated in 1982 Convention on the Law of the Sea – has been estimated to cost around US$ 4 billion, presumably based on the value of fish illegally caught by foreign trawlers.[28] Like these figures, the estimates of the total annual economic cost of piracy world-wide are uncertain, but most recent realistic estimates seem to be in the range of around US$ 70–200 million,[29] corresponding to no more than a few per cent of Indonesia's losses due to illegal fishing. If Indonesia were to increase its resources and capacity for maritime security and surveillance in its vast territorial waters and exclusive economic zone, these and other problems facing the country – such as the smuggling by sea of drugs, arms and humans – would probably be given higher priority than the suppression of piracy.

If the estimate of an average haul of US$ 5,000 from a low-level armed robbery is applied on the micro level, these can obviously be tempting prizes for the perpetrators. In Batam, Indonesia, before the 1997 Asian economic crisis, an industrious factory worker could earn up to Rp 800,000 (c. US$ 320) per month including overtime. By comparison, one confessed pirate, Iwan Maryono, interviewed by the Indonesian news magazine *Tempo* in 1993, claimed that he got around Rp 600,000 (c. US$ 270) for participating in a low-level armed robbery. 'The profit from piracy is just additional money. For my every-day needs, I rely on renting out boats', he told *Tempo*.[30] According to Iwan, some of those participating received nothing at all, whereas others presumably got a great deal more. If an average raiding group consists of five pirates and the average haul is around US$ 5,000, each person may get somewhere in the range of US$ 500–700 after necessary expenses such as boat hire, petrol and, quite possibly, bribes to corrupt officials have been paid. Although not a great fortune even by Indonesian standards, it would be the equivalent of around two months' wages, including overtime, for a factory worker before the 1997 economic crisis – and probably somewhat more in the years following the crisis.

Against the background of the problems in reporting piratical attacks, the map of the geographic distribution of piratical activity outside port areas that emerges from the IMB/IMO figures should be treated with caution. Not only are the IMB figures under-representations; they also do not accurately reflect the relative levels of piratical activity in the different parts of the region because there is reason to believe that the problem of under-reporting is unevenly distributed. When the IMB estimates that it only records about half of the actual number of attacks, this is based on the suspected under-reporting by the masters and owners of registered commercial vessels. A more important, but less often recognised, problem is that the Piracy Reporting Centre only rarely receives reports of attacks against small local vessels, such as fishing boats and barter trade vessels. The owners and crews of most such vessels are unlikely to report an attack to the Piracy Reporting Centre because they are often not aware that it exists and, even if they are aware of it, are likely to have problems in communicating with the Centre due to language barriers and lack of access to such advanced communication equipment as very high frequency (VHF) radio and satellite telephones. Nor does the IMB put any systematic efforts into collecting information about attacks against non-commercial vessels. To the extent that such incidents are included in the Bureau's reports, they are generally high-profile cases involving high degrees of violence, the taking of hostages and/or hijackings.[31] It seems that the Centre mainly bases such reports on information collected in the mass media, primarily Malaysian media, given that the Centre is located in Kuala Lumpur. Compared with other countries in the region, attacks on small Malaysian boats, particularly fishing boats, are more often reported than attacks on small vessels of other countries in the region, such as Indonesia, Thailand and the Philippines. For example, in 2003, the IMB reported ten actual or attempted attacks on fishing vessels in Southeast Asia, seven of which involved Malaysian boats.[32]

The IMB's figures, however, still heavily under-report attacks in and around Malaysian waters, particularly off Sabah in eastern Malaysia. Iskandar Sazlan of the Maritime Institute of Malaysia (MIMA), a Malaysian policy research institute, has compared the figures of the IMB to those of the Malaysian Maritime Enforcement Co-ordination Centre (MECC) which is Malaysia's central coordinating authority for maritime law enforcement. In the period 1993–2000, the MECC recorded 230 attacks off Sabah, whereas the IMB recorded only recorded 22 attacks in the same area – less than 10 per cent of the number of attacks reported by the MECC.[33] For the Philippines, the situation seems to be similar. According to figures from the Philippine Navy and Coast Guard, cited by Admiral (retd) Eduardo Santos, there were 1,233 reported attacks in Philippine waters between 1993 and 2003. The IMB, by comparison, only recorded 144 attacks during the same period.[34] Figures are not available from Indonesian authorities, but it seems likely that there have been numerous attacks in the past on small fishing vessels and other local boats in the country's waters that have not been reported to the IMB.[35]

The IMB is well aware of the problem,[36] but with the main financing for the Piracy Reporting Centre coming from the international shipping and insurance industries, and since the Bureau is a unit of the International Chamber of Commerce, its main priority is – quite understandably – to report attacks against commercial vessels. Attacks against commercial vessels – even though under-reported by an estimated 50 per cent – are thus reported to a much greater extent than attacks against small local vessels. This bias is problematic for those who are interested in the problem of piracy and armed robbery as a whole and not only in its impact on commercial shipping. Combined with the inclusion by the IMB of numerous incidents of petty theft against commercial vessels in ports, mainly in Indonesia, the emphasis on attacks against commercial vessels has led to a somewhat inaccurate impression of the distribution of piratical activity in Southeast Asia (and probably in other parts of the world as well), with relatively much attention given to the problem in and around western Indonesian waters, particularly in the Straits of Malacca and Singapore, and relatively little attention given to the problem in the southern Philippines, eastern Malaysia and the eastern parts of Indonesia. This is not to say that the IMB is not doing a good job but just to point out that the figures and information which the Bureau provides only reflect part of the total problem of piracy and armed robbery against ships in Southeast Asia, and that further efforts are needed – for example on the part of the IMO – in order to gain a more comprehensive and balanced picture of the extent and geographic distribution of piratical activity in the region, as well as in other parts of the world.

In Figure 2 and Map 7, an attempt has been made to estimate, on the basis of information from different sources (including the IMO, IMB, UNHCR and cited figures from various law enforcement authorities in the region) the number of reported pirate attacks in different parts of Southeast Asia in the 25-year period from 1980 to 2004. The figures are partly extrapolated and their calculation involves a measure of uncertainty. They are, however, probably still gross underestimations, given that it is likely that around half or more of the actual number of attacks are never reported, neither to any national law authority nor to any international organisation. The map is also based on accumulated statistics and does not necessarily reflect the current situation; in the Gulf of Thailand, for example, piracy has not been a major problem since the flow of Vietnamese boat refugees ceased in the early 1990s. The purpose of the exercise, however, is to provide a more balanced picture of the distribution of all piratical activity in Southeast Asia over the past quarter of a century than most current piracy maps and figures, which almost invariably are based exclusively on the small share of attacks that are reported by the IMB. It also shows that the real extent of the problem is much

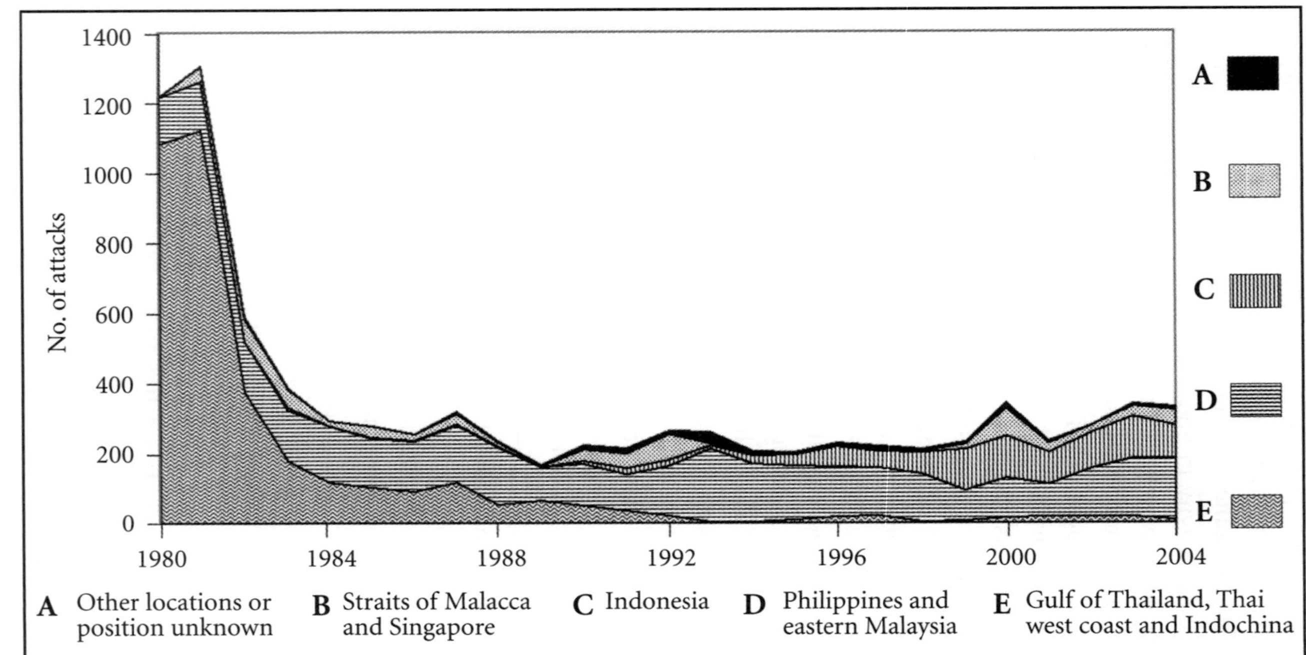

Figure 2: Piracy and armed robbery against ships in Southeast Asia, 1980–2004

Sources: See note 37 on page 109.

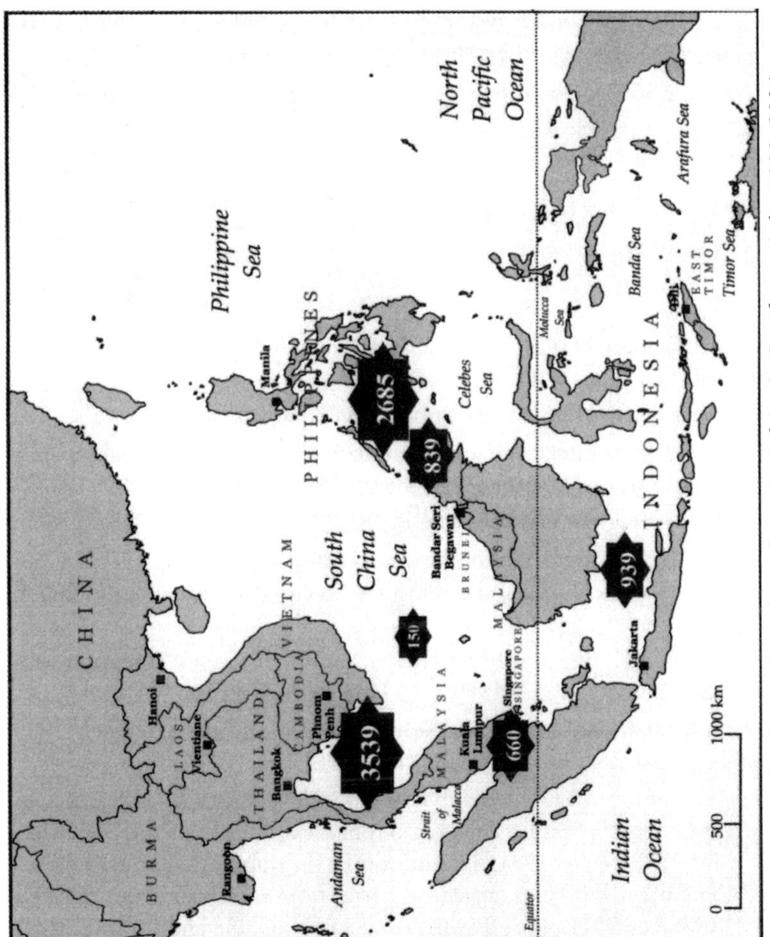

Map 7: Accumulated number of attacks against ships in Southeast Asia, 1980–2004

Sources: See note 37 on page 109

bigger than indicated by the IMB's figures, with a total of an estimated 8,800 reported attacks over the 25-year period, or on average around 350 attacks annually. If account is taken of the estimated number of attacks that go unreported, the figures should probably be doubled, giving a total of around 700 attacks each year in Southeast Asia.

Notes

1 See Ormerud (1924: 60) for a similar definition.

2 The literature on the legal aspects of the problem of piracy is relatively extensive; see for instance Rubin (1998) and Beckman (2002).

3 'Reports on piracy and armed robbery against ships. Annual report – 2004', IMO MSC.4/Circ.64 (5 May 2005), Annex 2.

4 ICC – International Maritime Bureau (2001: 1) and (2002: 3).

5 'Draft code of practice for the investigation of the crimes of piracy and armed robbery against ships', IMO MCS/Circ.984 (20 December 2000), item 2.2.

6 'Report of the Maritime Safety Committee on its seventy-fourth session', IMO MCS 74/24/17 (13 June 2001), item 20.

7 'Any other business: Piracy. Note by the Government of Sweden', IMO MCS 48/23/4 (10 March 1983).

8 'Resolution A.545(13) adopted on 17 November 1983. Measures to prevent acts of piracy and armed robbery against ships', IMO A13/Res 545 (29 February 1984). For the note by the shipping organisations, see 'Any other business: Armed robberies from merchant ships. Note by BIMCO, ICFTU, ICS, IFSMA, INTERTANKO, ISF and OCIMF', IMO MSC 48/23/7 (7 April 1983).

9 'Piracy and armed robbery against ships. Note by the Secretariat', IMO MSC 57/17 (1 February 1989), Annex, item 176.

10 'A report into the incidence of piracy and armed robbery from merchant ships', IMO MSC 48/INF.6 (6 June 1983), item 3.13.

11 'Piracy and armed robbery against ships. Note by the Secretariat', IMO MSC 65/16/Add.1 (8 February 1995), Annex p. 9.

12 'Report of the Maritime Safety Committee on its sixtieth session', IMO MSC 60/21, item 13.9. The Committee also invited member states to consider nominating competent authorities in their administrations to

receive and process reports of piratical attacks and to provide the contact details of those authorities to the IMO for the circulation to member governments; see ibid., item 13.12.

13 See ICC – International Maritime Bureau (1992a), 'Report of the Maritime Safety Committee on its sixtieth session', IMO MSC 60/21, item 13.7 and 'Piracy and armed robbery against ships. Note by the Secretariat', IMO MSC 60/13 (10 January 1992), Annex 1 & 2, and 'Piracy and armed robbery against ships. Submitted by Japan' IMO MSC 60/13/1 (14 February 1992).

14 *Straits Times* (28 February 1992); see also Abhyankar (2001: 168) about the launching of the Regional Piracy Centre.

15 Sutedjo (1992: 8).

16 ICC – International Maritime Bureau (2005a: 1).

17 The Inmarsat-C is a worldwide, satellite-based maritime communication system that is part of the Global Maritime Distress and Safety System (GMDSS), required to be installed on all cargo ships cargo ships of 300 gross tonnes and upwards and on all passenger ships on international voyages. Through the Inmarsat-C transmissions, piracy warnings and other broadcasts issued by the Piracy Reporting Centre thus reach the vast majority of international commercial vessels.

18 ICC – International Maritime Bureau (1997: 8 and 2000: 11).

19 For example, in 1998, the executive director of the IMB, Eric Ellen, estimated that around 40–60 per cent of pirate attacks were included in the bureau's annual reports; cited in Gottschalk and Flanagan (2000: 89).

20 'Reports on acts of piracy and armed robbery against ships. Annual report – 2004', IMO MSC.4/Circ.64 (5 May 2005).

21 ICC International Maritime Bureau (2005a: 29, 34, 41).

22 Interview with Stig Eklöf, first cook on the refrigerated carrier *Baltic Sea*, 1967, Gothenburg, 19 August 2005.

23 See ICC International Maritime Bureau (2005a: 4) and 'Reports on acts of piracy and armed robbery against ships. Annual report – 2004', IMO MSC.4/Circ.64 (5 May 2005). In the latter, details of the attacks and their location are given in the monthly reports on which the annual report is based.

24 It is assumed that the real number of attacks was twice the reported number, giving a total of 114 for the year in all of the Malacca and Singapore Straits. According to Ahmad (1997: 7) an average of 200

vessels per day transit the Strait, excluding intra-strait traffic, giving a total of around 73,000 transits annually.

25 Cited by Gottschalk and Flanagan (2000: 88). Higher estimates of the average loot from low-level armed robberies have also been suggested, for example by the IMB director Eric Ellen (1992: 22), who has estimated an average of around US$ 7,000. More recently, Mark Valencia (2005a: 80), based on press reports, has suggested between US$ 5,000 and 15,000. Even if the higher estimates are accepted, however, the cost is still negligible for the shipping industry as a whole.

26 For an estimation of the total worth of interregional trade passing through the straits, see Palma (2003: 5). See also Gottschalk and Flanagan (2000: 85–108) for a discussion of the cost of piracy world-wide.

27 Tempo Interaktif (27 January 2004).

28 *Suara Pembaruan* (31 October 2002). The problem of illegal fishing is not only short-term economic, but also has a long-term environmental impact as it contributes to rapid deprecation of fish stocks in the archipelago. The outfishing also tends to marginalise small-scale fishermen working with traditional equipment and boats and force them increasingly to turn to catching reef fish rather than pelagic species, often through the use of fish bombs that cause severe damage to the maritime environment. See further Butcher (2004) about the development of the fishing industry in the region.

29 See, e.g. Gottschalk and Flanagan (2000: 92) and NUMAST (undated: 11) citing a 1996 report by Lloyd's Shipping Economist. Unrealistic figures of US$ 16 billion, or even US$ 25 billion, are also sometimes mentioned, generally without any account of how such figures have been arrived at; e.g. Luft and Korin (2004: 61) and Warren (2003: 24). However, as Charles Dragonette (2005) has pointed out in response to Luft and Korin's claim that the annual cost of piracy would be US$ 16 billion, this would mean that the average haul of an attack would be around US$ 38 million (which more correctly, based on 332 actual reported attacks in 2003, should be US$ 48 million). Given that in most cases, the booty consists of either ships' cash or stores and loose equipment like paint, ropes and engine spare parts, such figures are obviously completely unrealistic, even if they purport to include the costs of increased insurance premiums due to piracy.

30 *Tempo* (28 August 1993).

31 For example, all of the 13 reported attacks against fishing boats in Southeast Asia in 2002 involved one or several of these actions; see ICC – International Maritime Bureau (2003: 26–47).

32 ICC International Maritime Bureau (2004: 27–44, 78–86).

33 Sazlan (2002: 13), citing the annual reports of the MECC. Perret (1998: 134) cites somewhat lower figures from the Malaysian marine police, but the figures cited by Sazlan seem more reliable, because he uses the first-hand reports of the MECC, which combines the information from different authorities, including the marine police and the navy.

34 Santos (2004: 3) and ICC – International Maritime Bureau (2004: 5).

35 For example, as mentioned in Chapter 4 above, the director of the North Sumatra Fishery Office, Ridwan Batubara, claimed in May 2004 that at least 30 vessels, including 15 Indonesian fishing boats, had been attacked off the coast of Aceh and North Sumatra since the beginning of the year; cited in *Jakarta Post* (10 May 2004). None of these attacks was reported by the IMB.

36 For example, the director of the IMB, Eric Ellen, told researcher Peter Chalk (2000: 60) that there were 143 pirate attacks in Philippine waters in 1993, resulting in the loss of at least 30 lives, none of which were recorded by the IMB.

37 Sources for Figure 2 and Map 7: Gulf of Thailand, Thai west coast and Indochina (Vietnam and Cambodia): 1980: Extrapolated, 1981–1988: Ellen (ed.) (1989: 282, 266 and 268); 1989–1992: Extrapolated; 1993–2004: ICC – International Maritime Bureau (2005a: 4). Philippines: 1980–1983: Extrapolated; 1984–1993: 'Piracy and armed robbery against ships. South China Sea: Report on IMO's fact-finding mission. Note by the Secretariat', IMO MSC 63/INF.15 (25 March 1994), p. 9; 1994–2004: Santos (2004: 3) with November–December 2004 extrapolated from January–October 2004. Eastern Malaysia (Sabah): 1980–1990: Extrapolated; 1991–92: Perret (1998: 134); 1993–2001: Sazlan (2002: 13); 2002–2004: Extrapolated. Straits of Malacca and Singapore: 1980–1981: Villar (1985: 118–120); 1982–87: Ellen (ed.) (1989: 247–271); 1988–90: Beckman et al. (1994: 33); 1991–92: ICC – International Maritime Bureau (1992b); 1993–2004: Ibid. (2005a: 4). Indonesia and Other locations or position unknown: 1980–1990: Annexes to the proceedings on 'Piracy and Armed Robbery against Ships' from the Maritime Safety Committee, IMO MSC 50–60 combined with Ellen (ed.) (1989: 247–271); 1991–1992: ICC – International Maritime Bureau (1992b); 1993–2004: Ibid. (2005a: 4).

CHAPTER 7

Piracy in the Name of God

PIRACY, REGARDLESS OF WHICH of the two major current definitions is used, is in principle conducted for the sake of private economic gain. Still, there are obvious political and religious implications in some of the piratical activity that over the past decades has occurred in Southeast Asia. In the Sulu region of the southern Philippines and the northeast coast of Malaysian Borneo, where piracy has been rife since the end of World War II, the situation has exacerbated since the insurgency in the southern Philippines started in 1972, and all of the major groups that fight or have fought for an independent Moro or Islamic state in the region have been involved in piratical activity. Such activity has often been justified with reference to the Islamist agenda of the perpetrators and organisations involved. Since the 11 September 2001 attack on the World Trade Center in New York, moreover, the potential threat of a maritime terrorist attack by Islamist extremists, particularly in the Strait of Malacca, has received much attention among security analysts as well as in regional and international media.[1] Against this background, the purpose of the present chapter is to evaluate the evidence of the involvement of Islamist groups and international terrorist networks in piracy and other forms of maritime violence and to analyse the underlying motives and objectives of these groups. What evidence and indications are there that terrorism and piracy are linked to one another in Southeast Asia and what are the potential threats of maritime violence, if any, that come from Islamist groups in Southeast Asia today?

With piracy rife in the Sulu region already in the 1950s and 1960s, it is perhaps unsurprising that insurgent groups in the southern

Philippines since the 1970s have turned to such activities as a means of fund-raising. During the earlier phases of the insurgency in the 1970s and 1980s, the first of the separatist groups, the Moro National Liberation Front (MNLF), attacked local fishing vessels in order to raise funds for the group's armed struggle. The MNLF also reportedly forced fishermen to pay protection money in order to avoid being attacked. According to a press report from 1988, fishermen in Zamboanga in Southwest Mindanao were forced to pay the equivalent of US$ 2,000 per month in protection money to the MNLF.[2] The other major insurgent group in the area, the Moro Islamic Liberation Front (MILF), which emerged in the early 1980s as a splinter group of the MNLF, has also been involved in piracy in order to raise funds and to procure resources, such as boats, for the group's logistic requirements.[3]

In addition to such piratical activity, both the MNLF and the MILF have also been accused of perpetrating maritime terrorist attacks. The definition of the concept 'terrorism' is contested, but for the present purposes, it will be understood as involving an act of violence, perpetrated mainly for political, religious or ideological purposes, that mainly targets civilians and the deliberate aim of which is to instil terror or fear in a population.[4] In this respect, maritime terrorism differs from most types of piratical activity – and indeed from piracy as defined by international law – as the primary objectives of piracy are economic rather than political, and violence is generally only employed as a means to those ends. By contrast, as regards terrorism, violence and creating havoc are the main objectives in themselves.

The evidence of MNLF or MILF involvement in maritime terrorism, however, is not conclusive and mainly consists of allegations of involvement of the two groups, or some of their members, in several violent attacks on passenger vessels in the southern Philippines. In 1983, the International Maritime Bureau, in a report to the IMO on the threat of terrorism to shipping, claimed that the MNLF was responsible for a bomb explosion on board the ferry *Santa Lucia* in Pagadian the year before.[5] Two people were killed and 50 injured in the attack. As regards the MILF, the group has been accused of involvement in at least two attacks. The first of these occurred in April 1997 when, according to the IMB, members of the MILF perpetrated an attack against a cargo ship, the *Miguel Lujan*, and an inter-island ferry, the *Leonara*, in the harbour at Isabela in the Sulu archipelago.[6] The attackers approached the two vessels in speedboats and sprayed them with machine gun fire. Five people were injured in the attack, two seriously, and panic erupted among the passengers of the *Leonara*. The other, more serious, attack occurred in February 2000, when a bomb exploded on the inter-island ferry *Our Lady of the Mediatrix* in Iligan Bay off Mindanao, killing around 40 people. The Philippine authorities blamed the MILF for the attack but no substantial evidence of the group's involvement was presented, and none of the perpetrators was charged with placing the bomb on the ferry. The allegations, moreover, were denied by an MILF spokesman who claimed that the organisation never targeted civilians.[7]

Since the start of the insurgency in the area in 1972, several coastal villages and towns in the area have also been raided by heavily armed marauders descending and departing in high-speed craft from the sea. Some of the most serious raids have occurred on the east coast of Sabah in Malaysia. In 1985 about 20 pirates, armed with M16 rifles and rocket launchers raided the town of Lahud Datu in Sabah. The raiders attacked the Standard Chartered Bank and the Malaysian Airline System office and shot dead ten people before escaping by sea with about US$ 82,000 in loot.[8] Another town in Sabah that has been raided on several occasions is Semporna. In the beginning of 1996, the town was raided twice within six weeks by armed men who attacked the police station using fish bombs and automatic weapons. In the second attack, the inhabitants were locked in the community hall while the raiders looted the town's shops and banks.[9] Four years later, in 2000, the town was again raided. According to Chin Ah Siong, a goldsmith, who for the second time had his shop looted: 'This time, the pirates were better armed. They had M16 rifles and even grenade launchers, and they numbered about 20. They stormed the town centre and shrieked like devils.'[10]

The precise identity and possible political affiliation of the perpetrators of these coastal raids have not been established, but eyewitness reports agree that they came from the Philippines, and Philippine authorities have accused members of the insurgent groups in the area of being responsible for the raids. The heavy armament and commando-style operations indeed indicate the involvement of some form of organised military or paramilitary group rather than loosely organised local bandit gangs.

Allegations of involvement in the raids have particularly focused on the third – but substantially smaller – major insurgent group in the area, the Abu Sayyaf Group. This strongly Islamist group, whose strongholds are in Jolo and Basilan, consists mainly of what Charles O. Frake has called 'outlaws with an agenda and an ideology'[11] – even if, as we shall see, the ideological character of the group seems to have been toned down in recent years. Compared with the MNLF and the MILF, the Abu Sayyaf has also since its formation in around 1990 been more closely associated with indiscriminate violence and the targeting of civilians, and it is the only Muslim insurgent group in the southern Philippines that has been designated by the United States Department of State as a Foreign Terrorist Organization.[12] Through its founder, Abdurajak Janjalani, the Abu Sayyaf Group was from the beginning linked to the international terrorist network al-Qaeda, and in the early 1990s the group received both training and financial support from al-Qaeda through the mediation of one of its senior operatives, Ramzi Yousef, who is best known internationally as the perpetrator of the 1993 bombing of the World Trade Center in New York.[13]

The Abu Sayyaf Group's first known act of violence was an attack that can be readily described an act of maritime terrorism. On 10 August 1991 Abu Sayyaf members fired a grenade at a Christian library-missionary vessel, the *Doulos*, in the port of Zamboanga, Mindanao, in retaliation against the missionaries' alleged defamation of Islam. The attack left two people dead.[14] In the 1990s the organisation became known in the Philippines for a series of violent attacks, including a raid on the Christian town of Ipil in western Mindanao, which saw some 40 people killed. The organisation was also implicated in the bombing a Philippine Airlines plane and an aborted attempt to assassinate Pope John Paul II during his visit to Manila in 1995.[15]

The Abu Sayyaf Group only rose to international fame, however, after it split into two or three roving units and started to move away from its original political objectives towards more criminal activities following the death of its founder and leader Abdurajak Janjalani in 1998.[16] On 23 April 2000 members of the group raided the Sipadan Island Diving Resort off the east coast of Sabah. The guests at the resort had just finished their dinner when six men, armed with assault rifles and a rocket launcher, descended on the beach from two speedboats. Shouting in Tausug and broken English, the attackers robbed the tourists of money and jewellery before forcing ten of them, together with 11 staff, to swim to the boats a short distance off the shore. Once all were on board, the boats with the hostages – nine Malaysians, three Germans, two Filipinos, two Finns, two French citizens, two South Africans and one Lebanese – and their abductors took off towards Philippine waters.[17]

After some initial confusion about the identity of the perpetrators, the Abu Sayyaf claimed responsibility for the abductions. According to press reports, the group initially demanded the release of a number of Muslim terrorists from prison, including Ramzi Yousef who had been arrested in Pakistan in 1995 for his involvement in the 1993 bombing of the World Trade Centre. As the kidnappers realised the futility of pursuing this demand, however, they instead demanded a ransom to free the hostages. The ransom was initially reported to have been set at US$ 2.6 million, but as the drama unfolded over the following months and gained widespread international attention, it increased to as much as US$ 1 million for each of the foreign hostages.[18]

The raid on Sipadan was a huge success for the Abu Sayyaf. The group gained unprecedented international media attention as Western journalists travelled to the kidnappers' hideouts in the southern Philippines, holding interviews with the hostages in makeshift jungle camps. Projecting itself as a religiously motivated movement, the

Abu Sayyaf also drew sympathy from Islamist groups around the world. Financially, the operation was also a great success. Malaysian businessmen collected some US$ 5 million for the release of the nine Malaysian hostages, and through the 'mediation' of Libya, another US$ 10 million were paid for the release of the other hostages.[19] This kind of money enabled the Abu Sayyaf Group to acquire more weapons, and also helped the group to attract more followers.[20]

Probably inspired by the success of the 2000 Sipadan raid, Abu Sayyaf members seem to have been involved in a spate of piratical acts involving kidnappings for ransom in recent years. In 2001, three Americans and 17 Filipinos were abducted from a tourist resort in Palawan in the southern Philippines and held for ransom. On 17 June 2002 a Singapore flagged tug, *TB SM 88*, and barge, *Labroy 179*, were attacked close to Jolo by eight pirates in military style uniform, who fired at the tug boat before boarding it. They stole the boat's communication equipment and abducted four crew members, one of whom managed to escape shortly afterwards. The other three crew members were held as hostages on Jolo for six months before the Abu Sayyaf in December demanded 16 million peso (c. US$ 300,000) for the release of the three crew members together with four Filipino Christian evangelists who were kidnapped in August.[21] In October 2003, six workers – three Indonesians, two Malaysians and one Filipino – were abducted from the Borneo Paradise Eco Farm Resort on the east coast of Sabah. In this case, the hostages were less lucky than those abducted from Sipadan: five of them were killed when trying to escape.[22] In April 2004, three crew members of the Malaysian tug *East Ocean 2* were abducted in the vicinity of Taganak Island in the Sulu Sea and held for ransom.[23] In March 2005, another tug boat, the Malaysian-flagged *Bonggaya 91*, was attacked by five heavily armed pirates off the east coast of Sabah. Three crew members were abducted and two of them reportedly died in captivity whereas the third managed to escape two months later.[24] There are probably more cases in addition to these.

The Abu Sayyaf was also responsible for what for several months appeared to be the worst maritime terrorist attack in modern times.

On 27 February 2004, the *SuperFerry 14* left Manila for Baclod and Davao in Mindanao. About an hour after departure a bomb detonated in the third-class seating area, killing over 100 people. The incident happened several months after the Abu Sayyaf had warned Muslims not to travel on the Super Ferries because of an imminent attack. Shortly after the attack, a member of the group, Rodendo Cain Dellosa, was arrested for perpetrating the attack after having boasted about it to acquaintances in Manila. Dellosa admitted that he had placed a time bomb, consisting of a cardboard box with 3.6 kilograms of TNT, on board the ship and then disembarked before the ferry left the capital. In spite of this admission and the strong indications of Abu Sayyaf involvement in the attack, the Philippine government and police initially rejected the claims by the group that it was responsible and denied that it was a terrorist attack at all, possibly because of pressure from the ferry company. In October 2004, however, after more than seven months of investigation, the police concluded that the explosion indeed had been caused by a bomb. The investigation also revealed that one month before the attack the ferry company, WG&A, had received a letter, believed to have been signed by the Abu Sayyaf leader Khadaffy Janjalani (a brother of the organisation's deceased founder) demanding US$ 1 million for the company's unhampered use of the waters of Mindanao.[25]

The *SuperFerry 14* bombing illustrates the difficulties in distinguishing between maritime terrorism and piracy in practice. Just as other terrorist attacks against public transport around the world – including, in recent years, the March 2004 train bombs in Madrid and the July 2005 attacks on the London public transport system – the ferry bombing in Manila no doubt had the effect of instilling terror in the general public. Still, the Manila attack differs from the Madrid and London attacks in that the main motive behind it was economic – that is extortion – rather than political. In that respect, the *SuperFerry 14* bombing was similar to the organised pirate attacks and coastal raids involving kidnappings-for-ransom for which the Abu Sayyaf has become known over the past five years. Since the death of Abdurajak Janjalani, the organisation seems to have undergone a process of criminalisation with its followers today being more interested and engaged in organised criminal activities, including kidnappings-for-ransom, piracy, coastal raids and extortion, than in pursuing the organisation's original Islamist or political agenda.[26]

Even so, the potential threat of a terrorist attack from the organisation – as opposed to more purely criminal activities – should not be disregarded. The Abu Sayyaf, or at least some of its members, continues to maintain links with international terrorist organisations such as al-Qaeda and its affiliated Southeast Asian network Jemaah Islamiyah.[27] The kidnappings-for-ransom in recent years have, moreover, left the Abu Sayyaf financially strengthened and enabled the group to attract new followers and procure more weapons and other resources. The Philippine military, meanwhile, has only been partly successful in its attempts to defeat the group. An Abu Sayyaf-engineered terrorist attack – not least a maritime terrorist attack given the Abu Sayyaf's proven record of maritime violence over the past 15 years – targeting large numbers of civilians thus seems like a potential threat worthy of serious attention, perhaps not only in the Philippines, but also in the rest of Southeast Asia.

❧

In spite of the strong association between maritime violence and Islamic insurgent groups in the southern Philippines, worries over the threat of a maritime terrorist attack in Southeast Asia have in recent years mainly focused on the Strait of Malacca area. This is understandable as an attack in that area may have much more far-reaching consequences for global trade and the world economy than an attack in the Philippines or eastern Malaysia. Fears of a maritime terrorist attack especially in Southeast Asia rose on the security agenda after the attack on the French super tanker *Limburg* in the Gulf of Aden off Yemen on 6 October 2002, when a suicide bomber rammed the vessel with a speedboat packed with explosives, blowing a hole in the outer hull of the ship. One crew member was killed but, because the ship was equipped with double hulls, the attack failed to set fire to the ship's cargo of crude oil, which seems to have been the intention.[28]

The incident seemed to confirm fears that al-Qaeda had moved from targeting aircraft – a comparatively difficult undertaking after security was stepped up in the wake of the 11 September 2001 attacks – to attacking the softer targets that the shipping industry provided. Other indications of an impending maritime terrorist attacks were warnings, issued shortly after the *Limburg* attack by the United States Federal Bureau of Investigation (FBI), that terrorists might use divers to plant explosives on the hulls of ocean-going vessels. In December 2002, moreover, the *Washington Post* cited United States intelligence sources who claimed that al-Qaeda controlled approximately 15 cargo freighters that could be used to support the organisation's operations.[29]

The *Limburg* attack also coincided with an increasing concern for Southeast Asia in the context of the United States-led so-called 'war on terrorism'.[30] On 12 October 2002 – six days after the suicide attack off Yemen – a bomb detonated in the nightlife district of Kuta in Bali, Indonesia, killing over 200 people, most of them foreign tourists. The attack demonstrated that terrorists in Southeast Asia both had links to international terror networks such as al-Qaeda and the capacity for carrying out complex and highly devastating terror attacks.

Although to date no concrete evidence has been presented of connections between the piratical activity in the Strait of Malacca region and Indonesia on the one hand and regional or international Islamist terrorist networks such as Jemaah Islamiyah or al-Qaeda on the other hand, the establishment of such links began to look increasingly worrying in the eyes of security analysts and government officials in the wake of the attack on the *Limburg* and the Bali bombing in October 2002. As a result, piracy – even the low-level armed robberies that for decades have been rife in the southern Malacca Strait region – came to be seen as a serious threat to the security in the region and was increasingly conflated with terrorism in the discourse on maritime security in Southeast Asia.[31] However, even though piracy has come to be regarded, at least in theory, as a major security threat by the members of the Association of Southeast Asian Nations (ASEAN), the effects of the attempts to increase international cooperation to combat the problem have only just begun to be seen.[32]

Maritime security analysts in Southeast Asia have not focused so much on the type of attack that befell the *Limburg* – or the *Super-Ferry 14*, for that matter – in which terrorists target a passenger or cargo vessel with the aim of causing destruction to the vessels, its cargo, crew or passengers. Attention has rather been focused on another, more spectacular, type of possible attack in which terrorists might use a vessel or shipment for the purpose of attacking targets on land. A major scenario is that terrorists might hijack a tanker vessel with a cargo of volatile liquid compounds, such as liquefied petroleum gas (LPG) or liquefied natural gas (LNG) – both of which are more volatile than crude oil or most refined petrol products – and use it as a floating bomb against a major population centre, particularly Singapore, the most Western-influenced country and the closest ally of the United States in the region.

The threat of terrorists targeting tankers with volatile cargoes such as LPG or LNG does not seem to be imminent, however. Most vessels carrying such cargoes are relatively modern vessels equipped with robust cargo security systems. Furthermore, cargoes of LPG and LNG are not extremely volatile except during loading and unloading (both of which usually take place far from major population centres). As noted by a report produced by the Organization for Economic Co-operation and Development (OECD) on maritime security, it is thus 'relatively unlikely that a terrorist group could successfully rig the explosion of a LPG/LNG vessel's cargo'.[33]

Evidence of an impending maritime terrorist attack, moreover, has been largely circumstantial, consisting, for example, of video footage, found by American forces in Afghanistan in 2001, showing the movements of Malaysian naval vessels in the Strait of Malacca.[34] Much was also made in the media in 2003 by the claim, originally provided by AEGIS Defence Services, a private London-based defence and security consultancy, that terrorists in early 2003 had hijacked the *Dewi Madrim*, a small chemical tanker, in the Strait of Malacca in order to practice navigation. According to *The Economist*, which cited the AEGIS report, this would have been the maritime 'equivalent of the al-Qaeda hijackers who perpetrated the September 11 attacks going to flying school in Florida'.[35] Investigations by the IMB, however, proved the story to be baseless; the attack on the *Dewi Madrim* was in principle no different from any other low-level armed robbery in the area. Certainly, however, the publicity did draw attention to the AEGIS report, which sold at a hefty US$ 5,800 per copy.[36]

Probably the most conclusive evidence so far that terrorists in Southeast Asia might actually ponder targeting maritime objects was unearthed in December 2001 when Singapore's Internal Security Department arrested 13 Jemaah Islamiyah members for planning a string of attacks in the city-state.[37] The group had three major plans that had been developed beyond the preparatory stage. Apart from a plan targeting a shuttle bus used by United States military personnel and a plan to bomb Western government and commercial buildings, the group also planned to attack United States naval vessels stationed in Singapore. The targets of the attacks were not civilian, however, but military.

The 2001 arrests in Singapore gave no indication that Jemaah Islamiyah was planning to hijack a vessel and use it as a floating bomb. The claims that such plans would exist have so far mainly come from intelligence sources, and consist of rather general and unsubstantiated pieces of information. In August 2004, the director of Indonesia's State Intelligence Agency, Abdullah Makhmud Hendropriyono, claimed that senior – but unnamed – Jemaah Islamiyah operatives in detention had admitted to having contemplated attacks on shipping in the Malacca Strait.[38] United States intelligence officials, meanwhile, claimed to have intercepted communications between Jemaah Islamiyah activists revealing a plot to seize a vessel in the area using local pirates and use it as floating bomb against another vessel, detonate it in a port or use it to threaten the congested sea lanes around Indonesia.[39] Intelligence sources, however, should be treated with caution because they tend to provide only the information which they deem favourable to their objectives, and they have in the past not been averse to fabricating evidence or pieces of information to suit their purposes. Claims that terrorists indeed were plotting a terrorist attack using local pirates would serve to securitise the problem of piracy in the region and force the authorities to step up their efforts to curb the problem. It might also serve to justify a greater role of the United States in the maintenance of maritime security in the region – something which, incidentally or not, was proposed earlier the same year by the United States in the context of the country's so-called Regional Maritime Security Initiative (RMSI).[40] So far, there is little indication that terrorists have approached local pirates, neither the petty pirates of the southern Malacca Strait area nor the more heavily armed kidnapping bands of the northern parts of the Strait.[41]

In terms of potential scenarios, and in comparison with cargoes of LPG or LNG, bulk shipments of fertilisers seem to provide terrorists with a more suitable target. One of the most commonly used – and transported – artificial fertiliser components in the world is ammonium nitrate. It is generally considered a safe and stable compound and the cargoes carrying ammonium nitrate are consequently not equipped with the robust cargo security systems that tanker vessels carrying volatile products are. Ammonium nitrate, however, can be easily manipulated, for example by adding fuel oil, which makes it highly volatile and explosive. The substance has been used by terrorists in bombings throughout the world on several occasions since the 1990s. So far these have been confined to land-based targets, such as the 1993 attack on the World Trade Centre, the 1995 Oklahoma City bombing, and the attacks on the United States embassies in Nairobi and Mombasa in 1998.[42] Ammonium nitrate has also been used in terrorist attacks in Southeast Asia, including the 2002 Bali bombing and the 2003 bombing of the Marriot Hotel in Jakarta. The Singapore authorities, moreover, seized 17 tonnes of ammonium nitrate that had been procured by members of the Jemaah Islamiyah group arrested in the city-state in 2001.[43]

In Southeast Asia, the use of ammonium nitrate bombs has also a long-standing association with criminal elements in the southern

Philippines. Already in 1993, *Asiaweek* reported that the substance was used in the Sulu archipelago for bomb fishing. The distribution of the powder used to make the bombs was controlled by powerful Tausug syndicates which smuggled it from Sabah and 'protected' the fishermen in the area with 'Mafia-style bribery and force'.[44] The possibility that members of insurgent groups in the area, such as Abu Sayyaf or the MILF, both of which have links to international terrorist networks, might get the idea of using a shipment of ammonium nitrate to stage a maritime terrorist attack does not seem far-fetched – and perhaps even more likely than the possibility of terrorists using a tanker as a floating bomb in the Strait of Malacca.

In conclusion, the evidence that Islamist terrorists are plotting a maritime terrorist attack in Southeast Asia is mostly circumstantial. This, however, is not to say that the potential threat of such an attack should not be taken seriously by the authorities or security agencies. On the contrary, not doing so is almost certain to invite terrorists to carry out a maritime attack, as demonstrated by the failure of the Philippine ferry company WG&A to take appropriate security measures after receiving threats that an attack against its ferries was imminent.

The threat scenarios that so far have dominated the security agenda have focused heavily on the Straits of Malacca and Singapore and on the possible connection between local piracy in the Straits and terrorism in the region. The conflation of the two problems has led to an increasing securitisation of the problem of piracy. Regarding what is essentially a criminal problem as a security issue, however, may not lead to the deployment of the most appropriate countermeasures – especially not in the Southeast Asian context where international cooperation on security issues, as noted by Ralf Emmers, tends to be characterised by high-level rhetoric but accompanied by little concrete action.[45]

The focus on the Strait of Malacca region, moreover, has largely overshadowed the threat of a maritime terrorist attack involving insurgent groups in the southern Philippines. The Abu Sayyaf, in particular, has a demonstrated maritime capacity and a long record of maritime violence, including maritime terrorism, piracy, coastal raiding, extortion and kidnappings-for-ransom. The organisation has also been relatively successful in recent years in increasing its number of followers as well as its financial resources and capacity for launching violent attacks. Even though in recent years, under the leadership of Khadaffy Janjalani, the Abu Sayyaf has moved towards more criminal activity, it still formally adheres to its original Islamist agenda and at least some of its leading members appear to entertain contacts with international terrorist networks such as the Jemaah Islamiyah. The possibility of a maritime terrorist attack orchestrated by the Abu Sayyaf – or another, old or new, group associated with the insurgency in the southern Philippines – thus seems relatively likely.

So far, the blending of Islamist political aspirations and piratical activity in Southeast Asia has largely been confined to the southern Philippines. Whereas maritime terrorism seems to have been used occasionally by all the major insurgent groups in the area since the 1970s, the main importance of the Islamist agenda has been to provide a measure of coherence among some of those purportedly Islamic groups involved in piracy in the Sulu region. However, piratical activity, as we have seen, has a long history in the region and was prolific even before the start of the armed insurgency in 1972. Providing 'an agenda and an ideology' to the outlaws of the region, the Abu Sayyaf seems to have created, or perhaps reinforced, a sense of unity and shared purpose among its members of outlaws. In that context, Moro nationalism, Islam and the idea of a global *jihad* provide, as it were, a moral justification for piratical activity and other forms of banditry.

The result has been that piracy and coastal raiding, which previously during the post-colonial period was less organised and more opportunistic, have become more sophisticated, involving well-planned and executed armed raids, extortion directed at major national companies, protracted negotiations for ransom and well-managed international publicity exercises. In these respects, the Abu Sayyaf resembles more an organised crime syndicate than an armed Islamist secessionist group. In terms of the threat that the group poses to maritime security, however, it should probably be regarded as both of these.

Notes

1 For some of the recent contributions, see Richardson (2004), Ong (2005) and the articles in Ong (ed.) (2006).

2 *Asiaweek* (27 May 1988).

3 Santos (2000: 3).

4 See Coady (2004) for a discussion of some of the major current different definitions of 'terrorism'.

5 ICC – International Maritime Bureau (1983: 4).

6 ICC – International Maritime Bureau (1998a: 12).

7 See Global Nation (Internet edition) (26 February 2003), available at the Internet web page http://www.inq7.net/globalnation/sec_new/2003/feb/26-03.htm, accessed on 25 June 2004. The MILF, has in the past generally not, as put by Peter Chalk (2002: 197), 'emphasized indiscriminate violence against civilian and non-combatant targets'. The group, or segments of the group, however, seems to have been involved in several violent bomb attacks in the Philippines in recent years; see International Crisis Group (2004: 11–12).

8 *Asiaweek* (27 May 1988).

9 *The Star* (24 June 1996) and Warren (2003: 18). See also *Berita Harian* (27 March 1996).

10 Chong Chee Kin (2000).

11 Frake (1998: 48).

12 See the list at Internet web page http://www.state.gov/s/ct/rls/fs/37191.htm, accessed on 23 September 2005. The only other major Philippine insurgent group on the list is the Communist Party of the Philippines/New People's Army, the activities of which, however, are mainly concentrated to Luzon and the Visayas. The NPA also seems to have perpetrated maritime terrorist attacks in the past; see ICC – International Maritime Bureau (1983: 4).

13 Williams (2003: 87–88).

14 Dépêche EDA (Internet edition), no 121 (16 November 1991), available at the Internet web page http://eglasie.mepasie.org/1991/novembre/philippines/121/depeche8_1/, accessed on 7 July 2004.

15 Frake (1998: 41) and Donnelly (2004: 5).

16 Ibid. (2004: 4).

17 *Asiaweek* (5 May 2000).

18 Ibid. and *Far Eastern Economic Review* (7 September 2000).

19 Ibid.

20 Capie (2002: 74).

21 ICC – International Maritime Bureau (2003: 19).

22 Manila Times (Internet edition) (29 October 2003), available at the Internet web page http://www.manilatimes.net/national/2003/oct/29/top_stories/20031029top5.html, accessed on 7 April 2004.

23 ICC – International Maritime Bureau (2005a: 19).

24 Ibid. (2005a: 19), 'Reports on piracy and armed robbery against ships. Issued monthly – Acts reported during March 2005', IMO MSC.4/Circ.67 (18 April 2005), and Manila Standard Today (Internet edition) (20 May 2005), available at the Internet web page http://www.manilastandardonline.com:8080/mnlastd/iserver?page=police01_may20_2005, accessed on 23 September 2005.

25 Manila Times (Internet edition) (7 April 2004), available at the Internet web page http://www.manilatimes.net/national/2004/apr/07/yehey/metro/20040407/met2.html, accessed on 4 May 2004; Time (Asian Internet edition) (23 August 2004), available at the Internet web page http://www.time.com/time/asia/magazine/article/0,13673, 501040830-686107,00.html, accessed on 16 September 2004; and Sun Star (Internet edition) (12 October 2004), available at the Internet web page http://www.sunstar.com.ph/static/net/2004/10/12/arroyo.orders. arrest.of.abu.leaders.linked.in.ferry.blast.html, accessed on 19 November 2004.

26 This also seems to be the conclusion of most observers of the organisation; see, e.g. Gutierrez (2000) and Donnelly (2004).

27 For example, in July 2003, two suspected Abu Sayyaf members escaped from the Philippine National Police headquarters in Manila together with a senior Indonesian Jemaah Islamiyah operative, Fathur Rahman al-Ghozi; see United States Department of State (2004: 27–28).

28 See ICC – International Maritime Bureau (2003: 20, 24).

29 *Washington Post* (31 December 2002).

30 E.g. Rosenthal (2003).

31 For a critical discussion of the discursive conflation of the two problems, see Young and Valencia (2003) and Valencia (2005a).

32 See Emmers (2003) for a critical discussion of the securitisation of transnational crime and the largely empty rhetoric which characterises much of the regional declarations and agreements on the subject.

33 Organization for Economic Co-operation and Development (2003: 12). See further ibid. (2003: 8–12) for an assessment of this type of threat.

34 *The Economist* (12 June 2004).

35 Ibid.

36 Liss (2005: 11).

37 See Ministry of Home Affairs of the Government of Singapore (2003).

38 *Jakarta Post* (25 August 2004).

39 The Telegraph (Internet edition) (12 September 2004), available at the Internet web page http://www.telegraph.co.uk/news/main.jhtml?xml=/news/2004/09/12/wterr12.xml&sSheet=/portal/2004/09/12/ixportal.html, accessed on 4 November 2004.

40 See further Chapter 8.

41 As regards possible GAM involvement in the piratical activity in the northern Malacca Strait, it is worth to notice that the organisation has in the past rejected suggestions by al-Qaeda to set up training camps in Aceh and to be part of a united regional front of Islamist insurgent groups in Southeast Asia; see Sebastian (2003: 365).

42 Organization for Economic Co-operation and Development (2003: 12).

43 Ministry of Home Affairs of the Government of Singapore (2003: 13).

44 *Asiaweek* (21 April 1993).

45 Emmers (2003).

CHAPTER 8

Combating Piracy

SINCE PIRACY RE-EMERGED as a security concern for the international maritime community and the shipping industry in the 1980s, a number of efforts have been made, both on the part of the industry, governments and international organisations, to combat the problem. Even though the problem persists, it would be erroneous to assume that the measures have had no significant effect. Some forms of piracy – notably the organised hijackings of commercial vessels – have ceased or declined drastically, and in some geographic areas the anti-piracy measures adopted by shipmasters and the authorities have resulted in significant decreases in the number of reported incidents. Still, there are a number of obstacles affecting the efficiency of the efforts to control piracy and armed robberies against ships. The purpose of this chapter is to review the most important measures that to date have been taken to control piracy in Southeast Asia and to analyse why they have – or have not, as it were – been effective.

As regards measures that can be taken on board vessels, numerous guidelines to shipowners and crews have been issued by national shipping associations as well as international branch organisations and the IMO.[1] In spite of some variations and conflicting advice concerning certain details, most guidelines agree on the general principles for meeting the threat of a piratical attack. All vessels should thus have a ship security plan and all crew members should be well aware of the risks involved in a pirate attack and be trained to meet such a situation, including having designated secure positions on board. The security plan should also include practical measures on board designed to detect, as early as possible, an attempted boarding and to deter attackers from boarding. Such measures include enhanced surveillance and watch-keeping, illuminating the deck and the area around the ship at night, regularly sweeping the surrounding seas with searchlights, monitoring radar up to a distance of one nautical mile in order to detect suspicious movements of small high-speed crafts and installing physical barriers such as barbed wire. Constant radio watch should be maintained with relevant local authorities and on all distress and safety channels when transiting piracy-prone areas.

If boarding is attempted, the master can try to shake off the would-be intruders by heavy wheel movements thereby making boarding more difficult, although such measures cannot be used in narrow passages and heavily trafficked areas, such as the Malacca and Singapore Straits. Another measure which has proven successful in the past is the use of fire hoses to spray possible intruders thereby preventing them from boarding as well as swamping the pirates' boat and possibly damaging their engines and electric systems. If an attack is attempted, the maritime Rescue Coordination Centre (RCC) of the nearest littoral state should be informed immediately via radio. If the shipmaster has problems in communicating with the RCC or other authorities of the littoral state, the Piracy Reporting Centre of the IMB can assist in conveying the report and distress message.

If the intruders still manage to board, alarm should immediately be sounded and all entrances to the ship's superstructure – especially those that provide access to critical areas such as the bridge, engine room, officers' cabins and crew accommodation areas – should be locked. Most guidelines, however, do not recommend that the crew resist the pirates unless the crew are superior in number and the pirates are unarmed. The use of firearms by the crew is generally strongly discouraged. According to the IMO's guidelines:

> Carriage of arms on board ship may encourage attackers to carry firearms thereby escalating an already dangerous situation, and any firearms on board may themselves become an

> attractive target for an attacker. The use of firearms requires special training and aptitudes and the risk of accidents with firearms carried on board ship is great. In some jurisdictions, killing a national may have unforeseen consequences even for a person who believes he has acted in self defence.[2]

The use of professional security guards on board has been recommended by some branch organisations,[3] and the threat of piracy and maritime terrorism has in recent years created an expanding market for private security companies, the credibility of which, however, in many cases seems dubious.[4] For most shipping companies, moreover, employing private security firms is not a realistic option because, once again, the use of armed guards may escalate the violence, and the costs involved are relatively high in relation to the costs and risks of piracy for the shipowner.

An important reason why piracy against commercial ships has resurfaced since around 1980 is probably the drastic decline in crew size on these vessels. Whereas most commercial ships in international traffic in the 1960s had a crew of around 40 people or more, even large vessels now typically have around 20 crew members or less.[5] Not only does this make it easier for pirates to seize a vessel; it also makes it difficult for masters to assign crew members to additional surveillance duties. On the other hand, some technical innovations may compensate for the smaller number of crew members. There are several tracking systems that allow shipowners to monitor the movements of their vessels via the Internet, thus facilitating the recovery of a hijacked vessel. Another, more recent, invention is Inventus UAV (unmanned aerial vehicle), which consists of a small remote controlled aerial vehicle equipped with cameras used for surveying the surrounding ocean for suspicious craft.[6]

One of the most effective devices is Secure-Ship, which consists of an easily collapsible electric fence that is mounted around the ship and gives the potential intruder a non-lethal 9,000-volt electric shock. If the fence is tampered with, an alarm will also go off, activating floodlights and a loud siren.[7] However, in spite of the relatively low cost and easy handling, it seems that most shipowners are reluctant to equip their vessels with the electric fence system and, according to the IMB, it has not sold very well.[8]

Another, less sophisticated but perhaps efficient measure to deter pirates is fitting a dummy on deck, as recounted by John Burnett.[9] According to a Riau-based informant to *Tempo* in 1993 with good contacts among the pirates in the area, fitting such a dummy – or even a dummy of a dog – on deck would be enough to deter them.[10] The impression among the pirates seems to be that shipowners do not make very serious efforts to protect their vessels and that they actually do not mind paying a 'tribute' when they pass through the Malacca Strait. As a Riau-based pirate told *Asiaweek* in 1988: 'These shipowners are very rich. While they're passing through the straits we ask them for a donation. It's like a toll. We don't carry guns and we never injure anyone. We just accept whatever money they give us. If they have no money, we leave.'[11]

The accounts of many pirate attacks indeed seem to confirm the impression that many shipowners and masters do relatively little to protect themselves from an attack. Often, pirates are able to board the ship and make their way to the unlocked master's cabin or bridge without being detected, and extra watches seem rarely to be assigned when ships pass through piracy-prone areas. On several occasions, pirates have been able to steal not merely large sums of money but indeed the whole safe containing the ship's cash – apparently because it has not been properly fitted.

Apart from the apparently lax security on board many vessels, the weakness and limited capacity of the marine law enforcement authorities – navy, coastguard and marine police – in the littoral states in Southeast Asia is an obvious reason why piracy persists in the region. The problem is most obvious as regards Indonesia and the Philippines, the two poorest countries in maritime Southeast Asia with the longest coastlines and largest territorial waters. In the southern Philippines, the central government has since independence in 1946 never had more than tenacious control at best. With the growth of organised criminal activity, including smuggling and piracy in the decades following World War II, the capacity of the authorities to uphold law and order, on the sea as well as on land, in the region declined further. For example, when a delegation of British and Philippine naval officers in March 1963 visited the Sulu region, they were not even allowed to stay overnight in Jolo because their Filipino hosts could not guarantee their safety on the island – even though the party throughout its visit in the region was accompanied by armed guards.[12] According to a British report of the visit, Sulu Province presented a 'depressing picture of a civil authority unequipped legally, militarily, or politically to cope with its internal security situation'.[13] The Philippine Constabulary, which had the main responsibility for maintaining law and order in the province, was found to be heavily understaffed and lacked necessary equipment, including wireless communication and launches, as well as coordinated intelligence. The Constabulary was also plagued by low morale, both because its officers feared for their own safety should they move against the pirates and other outlaws in the region, and because of corruption in several high places. In Tawi-tawi, the local commander of the Constabulary was widely believed – even by his superiors – to be in collusion with the most notorious pirate leader in the area, a fearful one-eyed bandit named Amak who was responsible for several pirate attacks and armed raids on settlements in North Borneo in the early 1960s.[14]

Throughout the post-colonial era, efforts to suppress piracy in the Sulu region have also been hampered by mutual suspicions and concerns over national sovereignty on the part of, on the one hand, the Philippines, and on the other hand, the British colonial administration in North Borneo (Sabah) until 1963 and, thereafter, the Malaysian government. One year before Malaysia was formed from the former British territories of Malaya (the Malay peninsula), Singapore, Sabah and Sarawak, in June 1962, the Philippine President Diosdado Macapagal unexpectedly announced his country's claim to the territory of British North Borneo, based on the Sultan of Sulu's alleged sovereignty over the territory in the nineteenth century. The friction between Malaysia and the Philippines over Sabah increased at the end of the 1960s, when President Ferdinand Marcos tried to launch an armed infiltration into the Malaysian territory. In the 1970s, moreover, the Philippines accused Malaysia of supporting the Moro insurgency in the southern Philippines by allegedly allowing the rebels to use Sabah as a base and training ground.[15]

These conflicts effectively ruled out any attempts at cooperation in maritime security between Malaysia and the Philippines in the 1960s and 1970s. In fact, when the Philippines in 1979 suggested a border agreement between the two countries to fight piracy, Malaysian officials answered by directly accusing the Philippine military of being involved in piracy against Malaysian vessels. According to Sabah's Chief Minister Datuk Harris Saleh, Philippine military personnel had become pirates and were 'harassing our people, especially fishermen and coastal ships'.[16]

Since the 1980s, however, the Philippine claim to Sabah has been toned down (although not yet formally revoked), and more cordial relations between the two neighbours have been established, largely within the framework of ASEAN. In the 1990s Malaysia and the Philippines even began to make coordinated efforts aimed at suppressing piracy in the region. A Border Patrol Co-ordinating Group, consisting of military officials from the two countries, held its first meeting in 1994, and in November the same year Malaysian and Philippine law enforcement personnel staged a week-long joint border patrol operation. Such meetings and joint exercises have since been held regularly.[17] These measures, together with increased efforts on the part of the Malaysian authorities to suppress piratical activity in the waters off Sabah, have in recent years resulted in a sharp decline in the number of reported attacks, at least in Malaysian waters. From a high of 57 reported attacks off Sabah in 1995, there were only nine attacks in 2001 according to Malaysia's Maritime Enforcement Co-ordination Centre, and the numbers have probably decreased further since then.[18] The problem, however, seems only to have been pushed more towards the Philippines, and figures suggest that piracy has increased significantly in the country as a whole in recent years.[19]

With much of the piratical activity closely linked to the insurgency in the southern Philippines, the government and the military seem to regard the problem as a security issue, and it is given a relatively high priority. However, the recent military efforts to defeat the Abu Sayyaf and other insurgent groups may actually have contributed to exacerbating the problem of piracy and the threat of maritime terrorism. Thus Eduardo Santos has observed:

> The unresolved insurgency and separatism in the country may contribute to the prevalence of piracy as rebels will increasingly look to piracy as [an] alternative financing scheme while conventional sources of funds start to dry up due to efforts to clamp down on terrorism. Meanwhile, as anti-terrorism campaigns heat-up on the ground, terrorists may look towards the sea to carry out their political agenda.[20]

In contrast to the Philippines, the Indonesian government does not seem to regard piracy as a security threat – possibly with the exception of the piratical activity off Acehnese waters in recent years, for which the Indonesian military, as we have seen, held the Free Aceh Movement (GAM) responsible. As regards the rest of the Indonesian archipelago, piracy consequently has a relatively low priority for the Indonesian marine law enforcement authorities – especially in view of the many other challenges in the realm of maritime law enforcement facing the country's overstretched naval forces, including smuggling and poaching. However, even though Indonesia has become something of an international whipping-boy for not doing enough to combat piracy, the impression that the Indonesian authorities, as well as the authorities of the other littoral states in the region, have ignored, and continue to ignore, the problem of piracy in and around their territorial waters is not entirely correct (see Figure 3).

In the early 1980s, when piracy in the southern Malacca Strait region first surged, it was reportedly an unwritten rule among the pirates not to attack Indonesian vessels, and no such attacks were

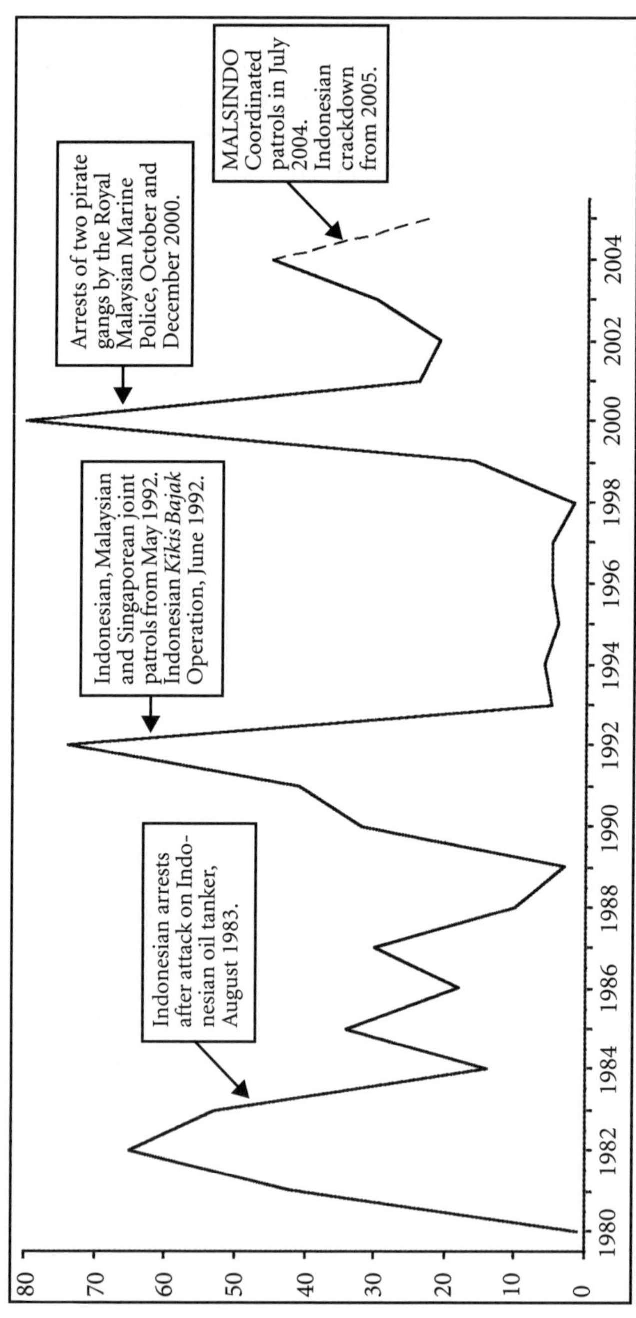

Figure 3: Piracy and armed robbery against ships in the Straits of Malacca and Singapore, 1980–2005

Sources: 1980–1981: Villar (1985: 118); 1982–1987: Ellen (ed.) (1989: 247–271); 1988–1990: Beckman et al. (1994: 33); 1991–1992: ICC – International Maritime Bureau (1992b); 1993–2004: ibid. (2005a: 4); 2005: Extrapolated from ibid. (2005b: 5).

reported between 1981 and mid-1983.[21] This strategy on the part of the pirates was probably not so much due to patriot-ism as self-preservation – or perhaps, as suggested by Admiral (retd) Sunardi, a former commander in the Indonesian navy, the circum-stance that Indonesian commercial vessels generally carried less cash than foreign vessels.[22] Coincidental or not – it may also have been prompted by the attention given to the problem in the Maritime Safety Committee of the IMO at its 48th session a few months earlier – the first crackdown on piratical activity by the Indonesian authorities came shortly after the first reported attack on an Indonesian vessel in the area, an oil tanker which was robbed of US$ 15,000 in the Phillip Channel in August 1983. Five pirates, believed to have been responsible for several attacks in the area, were arrested in Batam for the attack and over the following seven months there were no reported attacks in the Strait of Malacca area.[23]

The lull in piratical activity was not sustained, however, and in the course of 1984 attacks resumed in the southern parts of the Malacca Strait and the Singapore Strait, although not with as much frequency as during the early years of the 1980s. During the rest of the 1980s there were on average around 20 reported attacks each year, less than a third of the number recorded in 1982, the peak year. The numbers declined even further towards the end of the decade, and neither the Indonesian authorities nor the international community seemed to regard piracy in the region as a major problem anymore.[24]

In the beginning of the 1990s piracy surged again and reached unprecedented levels in Southeast Asia, particularly in the Malacca and Singapore Straits. The coastal states of the Straits were invited to advise the Maritime Safety Committee of what measures they were taking to suppress piratical activity in the area, and they were pressured in the Committee to enhance regional cooperation and adopt joint plans of action for combating piracy and armed robbery against ships in the region.[25] Obviously responding to the pressure, Indonesia, Malaysia and Singapore in May 1992 launched a co-ordinated patrol in the area, and in July the same year Indonesia and

Singapore signed a bilateral agreement providing for information sharing and coordinated patrols in the Singapore Strait and the Phillip Channel. The agreement – the full contents of which were confidential – also reportedly included procedures for the vessels of one state to obtain permission to pursue suspected pirates into the territorial waters of the other state, so-called 'hot pursuit', although this possibility, so far, seems not to have been used in practice. At the end of the year, a similar bilateral agreement was signed between Indonesia and Malaysia.[26]

Probably even more important in suppressing piracy in the Malacca and Singapore Straits, however, was the so-called 'Operation eroding the pirates' (*Operasi Kikis Bajak*) launched by the Indonesian navy in June 1992. Its efforts were concentrated to the Riau archipelago south of the Singapore Strait, where most of the pirates seemed to have their bases. The operation included intensified naval patrolling in Indonesian waters as well intelligence operations aimed at restraining or arresting the perpetrators. Dozens of pirates were arrested in Riau, many of whom were convicted and sentenced to prison terms of up to several years for direct or indirect involvement in the raids.[27]

The efficiency and resolution of the 1992 crackdown indicated that it had been ordered from the highest political level.[28] The speed and apparent ease with which the bilateral agreements with Singapore and Malaysia had been accomplished also indicated that the Indonesian government was serious in its commitment to eradicate piracy in and around its waters. Cynics among the pirates themselves alleged that the reason for the crackdown was that a ship belonging to Tien Suharto, the wife of Indonesia's President Suharto, had been attacked,[29] but probably more credible was the official explanation that the campaign was launched because the activities of Indonesian-based pirates in the Strait of Malacca area had begun to affect the nation's international reputation, giving a bad impression of the state of stability and security in the country.[30] This bad reflection, moreover, came at a time when Indonesia seemed to be particularly sensitive about its international reputation. The shooting by Indonesian security forces of hundreds of unarmed demonstrators in the East Timorese capital of Dili in November 1991 had led to massive international criticism, and in September 1992, Indonesia was scheduled to host the tenth summit meeting of the Non-Aligned Movement (NAM) in Jakarta.[31] Against this background, the Indonesian government was probably particularly keen to brush up the country's international reputation.

The result of the *Kikis Bajak* operation, combined with the coordinated patrols, was a drastic decline in piratical activity, and there were no reported attacks in the area in the last four months of 1992.[32] In comparison with the crackdown in 1984, moreover, the suppression of piratical activity in the region was better sustained for several years, and between 1993 and 1998, there were on average less than eight reported attacks per year. Piracy also seems to have been relatively well controlled in other parts of Indonesia up until the end of the rule of President Suharto in May 1998, and there were on average less than ten reported attacks per year in Indonesian waters – excluding thefts and robberies in port areas – during the period from 1993 to 1997.[33]

The relative control that the Indonesian authorities thus seemed to have over the situation came to an end late in 1998. In December 1998 alone, the IMB recorded 15 attacks in Indonesian waters, and the upward trend continued in the following year, when the number of attacks almost doubled compared with 1998, reaching an all-time high of 115 recorded attacks. Attacks in port areas increased by 47 per cent in the two years from 1997 to 1999, but the largest part of the increase was due to a spectacular increase in reported attacks on steaming vessels, which more than quadrupled, from 11 in 1997 to 49 in 1999. Piracy in the Strait of Malacca – outside Indonesian territorial waters but mainly perpetrated by pirates operating from Indonesian land-bases – also multiplied from three reported attacks in 1998 to 19 in 1999 and rising to a record number of 91 attacks in 2000.[34]

Since the surge in piracy in and around Indonesian waters followed in the wake of the 1997–1998 Indonesian economic crisis, analysts have often blamed the crisis, with its soaring unemployment rates and declining living standards, for the upsurge in piratical activity.[35] As a direct explanation, however, the economic crisis is not entirely convincing because the number of reported pirate attacks did not increase before the end of 1998, more than a year after the onset of the crisis.[36] For most of 1998 – by far the worst year in terms of economic hardships in Indonesia – there was no increase in the number of reported attacks in and around Indonesian waters.

Indirectly, however, the economic crisis was probably of some significance because it brought with it declining financial resources and a deterioration in the capacity of the Indonesian maritime authorities to maintain law and order in the country's waters. Comprising the world's largest archipelago with over 13,000 islands and a combined coastline of around 81,000 kilometres, a distance twice as long as the equatorial circumference of the earth, Indonesia's maritime law enforcement capacity was insufficient even before the crisis. Maintaining law and order in the vast archipelago includes, not only patrolling the country's territorial waters, but also the nearby international shipping lanes and Indonesia's vast 200-mile exclusive economic zone as regulated by the 1982 United Nations Convention on the Law of the Sea (UNCLOS).[37] The problem of adequately policing the vast archipelago has on several instances over the past years been pointed out by the Indonesian delegation in Maritime Safety Committee of the IMO,[38] but the problem seems to have been exacerbated since the 1997 economic crisis which brought about substantial cuts in military spending. According to a spokesman for the Indonesian navy, the country had only 31 operating patrol vessels in 2001, representing less than one-tenth of the estimated 350–400 ships needed to efficiently patrol the archipelago.[39]

The political developments in the country following the fall of the authoritarian and strongly centralised government of President Suharto in May 1998 contributed further to exacerbate the situation. The decentralisation that followed on the regime change in Jakarta meant that local and regional military commanders became, in practice, often more autonomous, and to some extent that central command structures became less important. The level of coordination and cooperation between the various maritime authorities charged with upholding law and order on the sea also declined. Both before and after the fall of Suharto, the main responsibility for maritime law enforcement in Indonesia lay with the navy, assisted by three other authorities: the Marine Police, the Directorate-General of Customs and Excise and the Directorate-General of Sea Communications. Under Suharto, these were coordinated by the Maritime Security Coordinating Agency, Bakorkamla (Badan Koordinasi Keamanan Laut), which was led by the commander-in-chief of the armed forces. With the declining political influence of the military in the post-Suharto era, however, it seems that Bakorkamla more or less ceased to function, and coordination between the four main maritime law enforcement authorities deteriorated, further impeding the efforts of the government to uphold law and order on the seas.[40]

In spite of these problems, however, Indonesian authorities – mainly the navy – have in the recent past had some success in apprehending and arresting those responsible for piratical attacks in and around Indonesian waters. A wave of piracy in the Malacca Strait in early 1999 was curbed through the re-intensification of the naval cooperation with Singapore under the 1992 bilateral agreement and through the setting up of an Indonesian special anti-piracy crack-force as well as, reportedly, a piracy coordination centre at Indonesia's regional naval headquarters in Batam.[41] On New Year's Day 2000, the Indonesian navy arrested four pirates in South Sumatra who apparently were responsible for a spate of low-level armed robberies in the vicinity of Bangka Island in the preceding year. The arrests were instrumental for the suppression of piracy around Bangka, and in the following three years, only two attacks against ships underway in the area were reported by the IMB.[42] In December 2004, the Indonesian navy, acting on information provided by the Piracy Reporting Centre of the IMB, recovered a tug and barge that had been hijacked off the Riau coast two days earlier and arrested four of the perpetrators.[43]

Meanwhile, the Singaporean and Malaysian authorities have also taken a number of measures to bring piracy under control in and around their territorial waters. For Singapore, with its vulnerable location in the Singapore Strait and its heavy reliance on international free trade, the problem has long been given high priority. With its small territorial waters and well-equipped naval forces, the country has been capable of keeping Singaporean waters more or less free from piratical attacks for most of the 1990s and thereafter, barring a few minor incidents involving ships in port. Since 1992 the country's navy has also actively worked with its Indonesian counterpart in patrolling the international waterways in the Singapore Strait and surrounding areas – although 'patrol fatigue' seems to have lessened the efficiency of the patrols in the mid- to late 1990s.[44] Malaysia has also increased patrolling and other efforts to suppress piracy, both in the waters off Sabah and in the Strait of Malacca, particularly since piracy in the region surged in 2000. In particular, the arrests of two gangs of Indonesian pirates by the Malaysian Marine Police in the Strait of Malacca towards the end of 2000 were instrumental in bringing down the number of attacks in the area.[45]

International efforts to coordinate anti-piracy measures have also been intensified in recent years, particularly as a result of the securitisation – particularly on the part of the United States and its closest ally in the region, Singapore – of the problem of piracy.[46] Fears that terrorists might stage a maritime terrorist attack in Southeast Asia, possibly using local pirates, were, as we have seen, heightened in the wake of the almost simultaneous attacks in October 2002 on the French super tanker *Limburg* off Yemen and the bombing of the Sari Nightclub in Bali. Apparently dissatisfied with the inability of the littoral states in the Strait of Malacca in suppressing piracy and other forms of criminal activity and security threats in the maritime domain, the United States in 2004 launched its so-called Regional Maritime Security Initiative (RMSI) for the Asia Pacific. The idea was that the United States would take a leading role in improving international intelligence sharing and coordination as well as strengthening the capacity for marine surveillance and law enforcement in the region. The RMSI, however, met with suspicion from officials in the region, particularly from Indonesia and Malaysia. The negative impression of the RMSI in the region was reinforced when the commander of the United States Pacific Command, Admiral Thomas B. Fargo, reportedly said that the initiative might include the deployment of United States troops to safeguard the Strait of Malacca.[47] The prospect of United States naval vessels patrolling the Malacca Strait apparently triggered the Strait states swiftly to agree on enhancing their own naval patrols and international cooperation, and in July 2004 the Malaysia–Singapore–Indonesia Malacca Straits Coordinated Patrols (MALSINDO) was launched. The launching of MALSINDO was an attempt to take back the initiative from the United States and aimed instead to establish a regionally based multilateral maritime security regime. Whereas the door was kept open for other countries to participate in the initiative, its purpose was to counter the United States' attempts to take a leading role in the maritime security of the region.[48] Despite initial doubts about the effectiveness of the coordinated patrols, these and other measures taken by the Straits states – including an air surveillance programme (called 'Eye in the Sky') and a crackdown by the Indonesian navy (called 'Gurita') – managed to bring about a substantial decline in the number of attacks in the Straits of Malacca and Singapore in 2005.[49]

The proliferation of piracy in Indonesia since the early 1980s combined with the problems for the authorities in curbing the problem has led several observers to accuse officials of the authorities in question – particularly the navy – of colluding with the pirates.[50] Most of these accusations, however, are based on very loose circumstantial evidence and made against the background of evidence of the involvement of sections of the Indonesian military in other, mainly land-based, forms of criminal activities.[51] The Indonesian navy has also been accused of other criminal activities than piracy linked to the maritime environment, including smuggling and extortion.[52]

The main 'evidence' of Indonesian military complicity in piracy seems to consist of victim reports of the perpetrators allegedly wearing Indonesian military uniforms or using certain equipment, such as launches and weapons, similar or identical to those used by the Indonesian armed forces.[53] However, such evidence needs to be treated with caution, as it is unlikely that most witnesses and victims of pirate attacks are qualified to identify Indonesian military equipment or even uniforms as such. Moreover, thugs in Indonesia often dress in military-style attire, making it difficult for outsiders to distinguish between military personnel and street hoodlums. Against this background, Noel Choong, regional director of the IMB's Piracy Reporting Centre, claimed in early 2004 that the IMB had no evidence of Indonesian military involvement in piratical activity.[54] Although such lack of evidence does not exclude the possibility that individual members of the Indonesian navy, or other authorities, may have been, and perhaps still are, involved in some of the piratical activity in and around Indonesian waters, there is little to indicate that official corruption and alleged military collusion with the pirates would be a major factor in explaining contemporary piracy in the region.

Apart from the problem of naval overstretch, particularly in the case of Indonesia in recent years, a major obstacle for apprehending the perpetrators is that the law enforcement authorities often get the report of an attack after considerable delay – often several weeks – or they do not get it at all.[55] As we have seen, ship masters and shipping companies often choose not to report an attack to the authorities because doing so may result in costly delays in connection with police investigations. A further problem, according to Rear Admiral Yusuf Efendi, commander of Indonesia's Western Fleet which has the main responsibility for maritime law enforcement on the Indonesian side of the Strait of Malacca, is to get the victims of the pirate attacks to testify in Indonesia. Most of the witnesses are foreign nationals working on international commercial ships, and to get them to appear before an Indonesian court is likely to be both costly and cumbersome for the shipping companies. As a consequence, according to the admiral, the Indonesian authorities have in the past often lacked the evidence to prosecute alleged perpetrators even if the indications of their involvement in piratical activity were strong.[56]

The efforts to combat piracy are also hampered by fundamentally different views on who should bear the cost of policing international shipping lanes such as the Straits of Malacca and Singapore. Indonesia and Malaysia have repeatedly called for an international scheme to share the financial burden of patrolling the straits, something which, according to the former Indonesian ambassador at large for maritime affairs, Hasjim Djalal, has support in the 1982 Convention on the Law of the Sea.[57] In February 1992, Indonesia's President Suharto floated the idea of introducing a toll system for the international shipping passing through in the Strait of Malacca.[58] His initial idea was that such a toll mainly be used to protect the environment of the area, but as the problem of piracy gained increasing attention in the media and international forums in the course of 1992, the idea was expanded also to include fees to cover the costs of policing the Malacca Strait against pirates. The Malaysian government strongly backed the suggestion, and in September 1992 the country's deputy prime minister, Abdul Ghafar Baba, said that his country was willing to dispatch men to protect cargo and merchant ships from pirates, but that the shipping companies would have to pay for these services. He also bluntly told reporters that the shipowners seemed 'ungrateful', not appreciating the fact that they were allowed to use the Malacca Strait for free. 'These people seem to have come out with a theory that they make the profit and we come out with the money to keep the straits clean of pollution and pirates', the minister said.[59]

Both Indonesia and Malaysia have also raised the issue of cost-sharing in the IMO. For example, in reaction to an IMO report on the Strait of Malacca, Malaysia proposed in 1993 that the Organization 'encourage users [of the straits], in particular, and others in general, to contribute and to assist technically and financially the littoral States to ensure that additional safety measures can be implemented'.[60] The proposition that user states assist the coastal states financially and otherwise in policing the Strait, however, has found little support among the international community with the exception of Japan. With the country depending heavily on maritime traffic through the Strait of Malacca, both for its exports of manufactured goods and for its imports of petroleum and other essential commodities, piracy has increasingly in the past decades – especially since the last major upsurge in 1999–2000 – come to be seen as a serious security threat by the country. In order to improve maritime security in the region, in recent years the Japanese government has taken a number of initiatives in the form of bilateral aid projects involving substantial transfer of resources, including patrol vessels and other equipment for maritime patrolling and surveillance, and joint anti-piracy training exercises with the national maritime law enforcement authorities in the region.[61]

Even though the willingness to contribute directly to the cost of policing the Malacca Strait has so far been small on the part of the international shipping industry, the allegations, voiced by the Malaysian deputy prime minister, that the industry does not contribute financially to combating piracy are not entirely correct. Above all, the industry – or, rather, parts of the industry – has since 1992 contributed to the financing, through voluntary contributions, of the Piracy Reporting Centre operated by the IMB. The Centre's activities, as we have seen, have contributed to a greatly improved reporting of piratical attacks and enhanced attention to the problem in international forums such as the IMO as well as in the media – not always to the liking of government officials in the region.

In spite of the reserved, or even outright condemnatory, attitude of government officials in the region towards the Piracy Reporting Centre of the IMB, it has on several occasions been instrumental in assisting the law enforcement authorities in solving major cases of piracy. Apart from facilitating communication between the victims of pirate attacks and the relevant national authorities, the Centre has at various times provided crucial information for tracking down hijacked vessels. This part of the IMB's activities often takes the form of delicate intelligence work involving the paying of informants inside the organised syndicates responsible for the hijackings. Rewards for the recovery of a commercial vessel paid by ship owners through the IMB can be quite substantial – typically in the range between

US$ 5,000 and 50,000, but sometimes as much as US$ 100,000. As regards the many cases of hijackings of tugs and barges in recent years, however, the relatively low value of the vessels is an advantage for the pirates, since it means that the rewards for retrieving them will be much lower than for commercial vessels – typically not more than US$ 1,000–2,000, according to Noel Choong of the Piracy Reporting Centre.[62]

The Piracy Reporting Centre has come to function as the main international centre for sharing intelligence about piratical activity, much to the resentment of government officials in the region who feel that the IMB, as a non-government organisation, is not an appropriate vehicle for international cooperation and coordination between the national law enforcement authorities.[63] Recently, as part of a Japanese initiative to form a Regional Cooperation Agreement on Combating Piracy and Armed Robbery against Ships in Asia (ReCAAP) efforts have been made to set up an inter-governmental Information Sharing Centre in Singapore in order to facilitate international cooperation in the suppression of piracy. The agreement was concluded between 16 Asian countries – Bangladesh, Brunei, Burma, Cambodia, China, Indonesia, India, Japan, Laos, Malaysia, the Philippines, South Korea, Sri Lanka, Thailand and Vietnam – in Tokyo in November 2004, but has yet to be ratified by all signatories.[64]

❧

Since piracy first surged in Southeast Asia in the 1980s, a number of measures have been taken, both by the shipping industry and the authorities in the region, to combat the problem. Many of these have been successful and there is little doubt that the problem would be much worse had they not been taken. Essentially, however, the reason why piracy still persists is that the problem is not seen by most important actors involved as serious enough and that there is disagreement as to who should bear the costs of tackling the problem. Most shipping companies are apparently able to bear the costs of an occasional low-level armed robbery against their vessels and often seem to be little interested in improving security on board their vessels, especially if doing so will incur substantial extra costs. Although some shipowners and insurance companies have financed, and continue to finance, the operation of the IMB's Piracy Reporting Centre in Kuala Lumpur, any suggestion that the industry contribute financially – for example, in the form of a toll system for vessels using the Strait of Malacca – has, understandably, met with little enthusiasm. Nor have most user states – with the notable exception of Japan – so far been prepared to contribute financially to policing the Strait or to improve the capacity of the Strait states to do so.

As regards the United States' Regional Maritime Security Initiative (RMSI), launched in 2004, it was seen with suspicion because of the leading role that the United States looked set to take in securing the region, and it triggered the launching of a regionally based effort to enhance maritime security, the tripartite MALSINDO coordinated patrols in the Malacca Strait. However, if this and other recent initiatives (such as ReCAAP) to forge an efficient regional maritime security regime in the Strait of Malacca region are to be successful, they probably will require the dedicated support – including substantial financial and technical support – from the international maritime community, including the states using the Straits and, directly or indirectly, the international shipping industry.

For many of the Southeast Asian states, particularly Indonesia and the Philippines, the two poorest countries with the largest archipelagos, there are a number of more pressing maritime security issues – as well as other political, social and economic issues – than piracy. Neither country has the capacity to patrol their vast territorial waters and exclusive economic zones, not against pirates any more than smugglers or foreign fishing trawlers, and this, apparently, is a crucial reason why piracy persists in the region. The lack of capacity and the relatively low priority given to the problem of piracy by Indonesia and the Philippines are quite sufficient as explanations as to why it has not been eradicated, and the possible corruption and collusion with the pirates on the part of some naval and police officials – the evidence of which, moreover, in recent years has been largely circumstantial – does not appear to be a major explanation as to why piracy has not yet been efficiently suppressed in Southeast Asia.

Notes

1 See, e.g. Norwegian Shipowners' Association (1997), BIMCO (1998) and International Chamber of Shipping and International Shipping Federation (2004). The summary of measures provided here is mainly based on the IMO guidelines; see 'Piracy and armed robbery against ships. Guidance to shipowners and ship operators, shipmasters and crews on preventing and suppressing acts of piracy and armed robbery against ships', IMO MSC/Circ.623/Rev.3 (29 May 2002).

2 Ibid., item 46.

3 E.g. Norwegian Shipowners' Association (1997: 6–7).

4 See Liss (2005).

5 Committee on the Effect of Smaller Crews on Maritime Safety (1990: 1).

6 See the manufacturer's Internet web page at http://www.inventus-uav.com, accessed on 3 October 2005.

7 See Mukundan (2004: 6–7) and the Internet web page of the manufacturer, Secure Marine, at the Internet web page http://www.secure-marine.com, accessed on 19 March 2004. A drawback with the system, however, is that, for security reasons, it cannot be fitted on tankers and other vessels carrying flammable goods.

8 Interview by the author with Jayant Abhyankar, deputy director of the IMB, Barking, Essex, 9 February 2005.

9 Burnett (2002: 131).

10 *Tempo* (28 August 1993).

11 *Asiaweek* (27 May 1988). The observation that shipowners could do more to protect their vessels from pirate attacks has also been made by more initiated analysts. I. R. Hyslop (1989: 23) concluded that anti-piracy initiatives were inhibited by the 'practical economic insignificance of piracy on world shipping, and the consequent temptation to "rely on insurance"'.

12 'Anglo-Philippine naval cooperation: Report of a visit to the southern Philippines, 18th–21st March, 1963' (undated) [Annex C to 'Report by Lieutenant Commander P. A. Woolings R. N. on his visit to the Philippines 11th–22nd March 1963' (undated)], NA, CO 1030/1660.

13 'Situation in Sulu Province (mid March 1963)' (undated) [Appendix to Annex C to 'Report by Lieutenant Commander P. A. Woolings R. N. on his visit to the Philippines 11th–22nd March 1963' (undated)], NA, CO 1030/1660.

14 Ibid. and 'Anglo-Philippine naval cooperation' (undated).

15 For the conflict over Sabah, see Noble (1977) and Collins (2003: 134–135).

16 *Far Eastern Economic Review* (7 December 1979).

17 See *New Straits Times* (7 February 1995), *The Star* (14 November 1995), Manila Times (Internet edition) (24 June 2003), available at the Internet web page http://www.manilatimes.net/national/2003/jun/24/top_stories/20030624top11.html, accessed on 4 April 2004.

18 See, e.g. *Sunday Star* (11 January 2004). For the figures of the MECC, see Sazlan (2002: 13).

19 According to Santos (2004: 3), there were 87 reported attacks in 2001, 123 in 2002 and 155 in 2003. In the first seven months of 2004, there were 96 attacks, which, if spread over 12 months, would correspond to 165 reported attacks, or close to double the 2001 figure.

20 Ibid (2004: 14).

21 *Tempo* (28 August 1993). Of the 93 attacks listed by the IMB in its first report to the IMO on piracy and armed robbery against ships, none was against an Indonesian-flagged vessel; see 'A report into the incidence of piracy and armed robbery from merchant ships', IMO MSC 48/INF.6 (6 June 1983), Appendix C.

22 Interview by the author, Jakarta, 4 February 2004.

23 'Piracy and armed robbery against ships. A Second Report into the Incidence of Piracy and Armed Robbery from Merchant Ships. Note by the Secretariat', IMO MSC/INF.2 (10 July 1984), pp. 10–11, 13.

24 It is illustrating that in 1985, the outgoing naval commander of the Riau archipelago, First Admiral Aboe, did not mention piracy when he listed the threats to maritime security in the area. He did, however, mention numerous other threats, such as illegal fishing, bomb fishing, drug trafficking, arms smuggling, smuggling of various foreign products, infiltration, illegal immigration and the flow Indochinese refugees; *Sinar Harapan* (2 June 1985).

25 'Report of the Maritime Safety Committee on its sixtieth session', IMO MSC 60/21/13, items10 and 11.

26 'Report of the Maritime Safety Committee on its sixty-second session', IMO MSC 62/25/15, item 18, Beckman (2002: 330), *Straits Times Weekly Overseas Edition* (11 July 1992) and *Jakarta Post* (3 December 1992).

27 It is unclear from media reports exactly how many alleged pirates were arrested. According to the *Far Eastern Economic Review* (19 November 1992), 70 Indonesians were arrested between June and November 1992. Earlier the same month, the Director-General of Sea Communications Soentoro said that 48 pirates had been arrested and that the Malacca Strait was free from pirate activity; see *Suara Pembaruan* (7 November 1992). A few of weeks later, Admiral Yusuf Efendi said that 75 per cent of a total of between 100 and 200 pirates had been arrested. Because of lack of evidence, however, only 18 of these looked set to be prosecuted; see *Suara Karya* (3 December 1992). The following year, *Tempo* (28 August 1993) claimed that 37 people had been arrested under the operation.

28 For example, recognising the importance of Jakarta's political will to combat piracy, the director of the Hong Kong Shipowners' Association, Michael Farlie, observed that 'no effective of lasting solution to eliminate piracy in Southeast Asian waters can be accomplished without the direct interest of [Indonesian] President Suharto'; quoted in the *New Straits Times* (31 August 1992).

29 A pirate leader in Riau, quoted by Time (Asian Internet edition) (20 August 2001) claimed that this was the reason for the 1992 crackdown.

30 *Angkatan Bersenjata* (29 June 1992).

31 See Economist Intelligence Unit (1992a: 12) and (1992b: 10).

32 ICC – International Maritime Bureau (1992b: 4–5) and Beckman *et al.* (1994: 33). The collision in the Malacca Strait in September 1992 between the *Nagasaki Spirit* and the *Ocean Blessing*, however, may have been caused by piracy. There were no survivors of the collision, and the exact circumstances surrounding the incident remain unclear. See further Burnett (2002: 134–143) for a discussion about the possibility of piracy as a cause of the collision.

33 For the figures, see the annual reports of the ICC – International Maritime Bureau (1994–1997 and 1998a).

34 Figures based on ibid. (1998a and 1999–2001).

35 See, e.g. Chalk (2000: 61), Lintner (2000: 18) and Beckman (2002: 331). This was also the view of the IMB's director P. Mukundan as quoted in the *New Straits Times* (16 May 1999).

36 During the initial phase of the crisis, from September to December 1997, the number of attacks actually declined compared with previous months; see ICC – International Maritime Bureau (1998a: 17–22) and ibid. (1999: 20–26, 38–40) for the 1998 figures. Officials from the Bureau, moreover, did not at the time see any noticeable impact of the

economic crisis on the incidence of piracy; see Renwick and Abbott (1999: 191).

37 With 1.57 million square nautical miles of exclusive economic zone, Indonesia has the largest EEZ of all developing countries and the fourth largest in the world; see Sanger (1987: 66).

38 See, e.g. 'Report of the Maritime Safety Committee on its fifty-ninth session', IMO MSC 59/33, item 19.7

39 *Kompas* (21 December 2002). Mark Valencia (2005b: 105) has cited claims, reported in the media in April 2001, that the country then had about 115 ships, or about one-third of the required capacity. The figures vary, but there is unanimous agreement that the Indonesian navy is overstretched.

40 Interview with Admiral (retd) R. M. Sunardi, Jakarta, 4 February 2004. For the role of Bakorkamla under the Suharto regime, see Lowry (1996: 80). In 2005 the Indonesian Coast Guard was formed through the merger of the Marine Police and the Directorate-General of Sea Communications, reducing the number of authorities responsible for maritime law enforcement to three. It remains, at the time of writing, to be seen whether this will improve the country's maritime law enforcement capacity and coordination.

41 See *Suara Karya* (20 May 1999 and 12 July 1999) and *Suara Pembaruan* (2 September 1999). The IMB did not record any attacks against ships outside of port areas in the months from June to October 1999; see ICC – International Maritime Bureau (2000: 23–32, 43–45).

42 For the numbers, see ICC – International Maritime Bureau (1996–2003), and for the arrests, see *Republika* (6 January 2000).

43 ICC – International Maritime Bureau (2005a: 25–26).

44 Mak Joon Num (2006). The inefficiency of the coordinated patrols towards the end of the 1990s probably also contributed to the surge in piracy in the Malacca and Singapore Straits in 2000.

45 ICC – International Maritime Bureau (2001: 19); see also *Kompas* (17 December 2000).

46 Following the Copenhagen school of security studies, the term 'securitisation' is used here to signify a process whereby an issue, usually on the initiative of an elite actor or actors, comes to be regarded as a security threat thereby justifying extraordinary measures to deal with it; see, e.g. Buzan et al. (1998).

47 See Bradford (2005) about the controversy sparked by Admiral Fargo's alleged comments. See also the information about RMSI published by

the United States Pacific Command at the Internet web page http://www.pacom.mil/rmsi/, accessed on 3 October 2005.

48 For MALSINDO, see *Jakarta Post* (21 July 2004) and Mak Joon Num (2006).

49 ICC – International Maritime Bureau (2005b: 5) and Agence France-Presse (1 December 2005), available at the Internet web page http://www.defencetalk.com/news/publish/article_004319.php, accessed on 19 December 2005.

50 E.g. Vagg (1995: 75–76), Carpenter and Wiencek (1996: 83), Chalk (2000: 61), Beckman (2002: 317), Stuart (2002: 121–123) and Warren (2003: 22). In 1992, the *Far Eastern Economic Review* (2 July 1992) also reported that Malaysian and Singaporean shipowners suspected collusion between the pirates and some Indonesian customs officials.

51 See Ryter (1998) and Lintner (2003: 276–304) for the connections between the Indonesian military and criminal elements. According to Timo Kivimäki of NIAS – Nordic Institute of Asian Studies (personal conversation, October 2003), there is also evidence of involvement of the Indonesian army in road piracy in Aceh.

52 For example, when fishermen in North Sumatra in 2002 staged a demonstration to protest against the navy's apparent inability to protect their lives and property at sea, a spokesman for the fishermen claimed that security officials forced them to pay protection money, ranging from Rp 50,000 to 300,000 (US$ 8–48) per day, an allegation which was denied by First Lieutenant Arief of the Belawan naval base; *Jakarta Post* (13 August 2002). For indications of the involvement of naval personnel in smuggling, see Stuart (2002: 98).

53 E.g. *The Star* (1 December 2002).

54 Interview by the author, Kuala Lumpur, 16 January 2004.

55 'Report of the Maritime Safety Committee on its sixty-fifth session', IMO MSC 65/25/16.6. This claim has also been made repeatedly by Indonesian marine law enforcement officials in the media; e.g. *Suara Pembaruan* (5 November 1993) and *Media Indonesia* (13 July 2000). The deputy director of the IMB, Captain Jayant Abhyankar, agrees that this may be a problem, mainly because ship masters delay reporting and may have difficulties, because of language barriers, in communicating with the relevant national Marine Rescue Coordination Centre (RCC); interview by the author, Barking Essex, 9 February 2005.

56 *Suara Karya* (3 December 1992). A further problem with getting witnesses to testify is that many of them may fear for their own safety,

especially if the defendants are members of international criminal organisations. This was, for example, a problem in the trial, held in Mumbai, India, in early 2003 against the perpetrators of the *Alondra Rainbow* hijacking; Jayant Abhyankar, deputy director of the IMB, interview by the author, Barking, Essex, 9 February 2005.

57 Interview by the author, Jakarta, 30 January 2004. The claim is mainly based on Article 43 of the convention, which states that user states and states bordering a strait used for international navigation should co-operate 'in the establishment and maintenance in a strait of necessary navigational and safety aids or other improvements in aid of international navigation'. For the argument, see further Djalal (2005).

58 *Suara Karya* (14 February 1992).

59 *The Star* (2 September 1992).

60 'Piracy and armed robbery against ships. Comments on "The report of the Working Group on the Malacca Straits Area" (IMO). Submission by Malaysia', IMO MSC 63/17/2 (6 September 1993), item 3.2. Indonesia, likewise, recommended that the IMO assist the littoral states in implementing anti-piracy measures and other safety improvements deemed necessary in the Malacca Strait; 'Comments by Indonesia on the report of the IMO Working Group on the Malacca Strait Area', IMO MSC 63/17/2/Add.1 (undated), item 11.

61 See Bradford (2004). It is still too early, at the time of writing, to evaluate the effect of these efforts

62 Interview by the author, Kuala Lumpur, 16 January 2004.

63 Indonesia, for example, resented the recommendation, made by the IMO's Working Group on the Malacca Strait Area in 1993 that the littoral states immediately should inform the Regional Piracy Centre of the IMB of any piratical incident in the Malacca Strait area. According to the comments by Indonesia: 'As IMB's RPC in Kuala Lumpur is not an inter-governmental organisation but a Non-Governmental Organisation, this particular part of the recommendation is therefore not appropriate'; IMO MSC 63/17/2/Add.1 (undated), item 4.

64 As pointed out by Bradford (2005), a weakness of the agreement is that it only obligates governments to share information which they deem pertinent to immediate pirate attacks, and that the Centre's operation will depend on voluntary contributions. There also appears to have been some disagreement among the signatories as to where the Centre should be located.

CHAPTER 9

Conclusion

OVER THE PAST 25 YEARS, pirates in different parts of Southeast Asia have probably attacked over 17,000 vessels, or on average more than 700 per year, claiming the lives of thousands of innocent seafarers, from Vietnamese boat refugees to local fishermen and crew members on international commercial vessels. This horrendous record even makes the achievements of Blackbeard and his contemporaries close to 300 years ago look pallid; in an average year they captured and plundered less than one third of the number of ships that today's pirates in Southeast Asia do.

Piracy in Southeast Asia for the past few decades has been concentrated in a few 'hotspots' in the region. The most pirate-infested waters in the region – and possibly in the world – are in the southern Philippines, including the waters off Mindanao and the Sulu Sea, and the adjacent waters off Sabah in eastern Malaysia. This is a part of the region where piracy and maritime raiding have been practised by certain ethnic groups, often successfully, for centuries and it is also the part of the region where piracy first resurfaced in the immediate post-colonial era.

In terms of the number of attacks, the Sulu pirates were only dwarfed in the late 1970s and 1980s by their Thai counterparts as thousands of vulnerable Vietnamese refugee boats crossing the Gulf of Thailand provided ample opportunity for the Thai pirates not only to plunder but also to rape and commit other atrocities. The attacks in the Gulf of Thailand remain by far the most serious outbreak of piratical activity in Southeast Asia in modern times, and although they were gradually suppressed in the course of the 1980s, the attacks only ceased as the flow of refugees ended in the early 1990s.

From the early 1980s, piracy also resurfaced along some of the region's major international shipping lanes, particularly in and around the Straits of Malacca and Singapore, but also in other locations in Indonesia and the South China Sea. Although the attacks in these areas only comprised, and still comprise, a minority of the total number of attacks in the region, they have gained relatively much attention as, ever since the issue was first raised internationally in the early 1980s, they have come to be seen as more of an international security threat – both to international shipping and to international maritime traffic in general – than has the piratical activity in the southern Philippines or the Gulf of Thailand. The fundamental difference is that, whereas the victims of the attacks in the two latter regions were – and still are in the case of the southern Philippines – mainly local refugees, fishermen, traders and coastal dwellers, most of the victims in the Strait of Malacca region were – and still are – international commercial vessels and their crews. Both in the media and in international forums such as the International Maritime Organization, the interests of the latter have been much better represented than those of poor fishermen and other local pirate victims, especially if they are found in remote parts of Southeast Asia.

Various explanations have been proposed for the resurgence and persistence of piracy in the region since the beginning of the 1980s, including different economic, political, social and cultural factors. All too often, however, the arguments have been based on circumstantial evidence and associative reasoning with little attempt to establish the link between the phenomenon and the explanatory variables. Poverty, corruption and cultural dispositions are, for example, all factors that have been suggested as explanations as to why piracy surged in Southeast Asia from around 1980 but little attempt has been made to establish the causal link between piracy and the alleged explanations. Indeed, the empirical evidence is often lacking. For example, from what we know of the social and economic background of the pirates in Indonesia's Riau Archipelago, there is little to suggest that they would come from particularly poor groups in Indonesian society. The ways in which they seem to spend most of the proceeds of the raids – that is, on various types of conspicuous consumption – also suggest that, whereas economic motives obviously are central, poverty is not a major reason to take to pirating. Explaining piracy with reference to poverty, moreover, is not convincing unless it can be explained why piracy did not surge in Indonesia in the 1930s or the 1960s when poverty was both greater and more widespread than ever in the 1980s or 1990s.

Several observers have also raised allegations of official corruption or even collusion with the pirates on the part of the navies and other authorities in the region, particularly with regard to Indonesia and the Philippines. However, the evidence of such corruption – in contrast to the more extensively documented complicity of corrupt Chinese officials in piratical activity in the early 1990s – is mainly circumstantial and unsubstantiated, and even in the relatively likely case that there were to be some substance in the allegations, there is nothing to indicate that official corruption would be a major factor for explaining contemporary Southeast Asian piracy.

Nor do cultural explanations carry much credibility, at least not with respect to the Strait of Malacca region. Whereas piracy historically has been prolific in the region, there is nothing to suggest that there exists a historical or cultural continuity between today's pirates, regardless of whether they operate out of Aceh, Riau or South Sumatra, and the sea nomads (*orang laut*) who since the dawn of history and until the arrival steam gunboats in the mid-nineteenth century were the most formidable pirates of the region. Likewise, in the Gulf of Thailand, there is nothing to suggest that the Thai pirates in the 1980s – most of whom seemed to be opportunistic fishermen – turned to piracy because of any cultural predisposition or sanctioning of such activities. If anything, the plunder and atrocities committed against the hapless boat refugees seem to be in blatant contradiction to the humanitarian principles of Theravada Buddhism, which is generally regarded as a central pillar of Thai culture and society.

Only in the southern Philippines are cultural explanations relevant to explain why piracy resurfaced in the post-colonial era. In spite of sustained efforts during the nineteenth century, the Spanish colonial government in Manila never managed completely to suppress piracy and raiding in the Sulu region, and the Spanish never gained effective control over the southern Philippines. Under the American colonial regime (1898–1941), piratical activity was indeed suppressed, but the (nominally) Muslim communities of the southern parts of the archipelago, including the former marauding communities of Tausug, Samal and Illanun speakers, were never to any great extent integrated – economically, socially, politically or culturally – with the majority of Christian Filipinos in Luzon and the Visayas. Anthropological evidence from the post-colonial period suggests that the cultural sanctioning of violence and maritime raiding thus survived more or less intact through the relatively brief colonial era in the region, at least among some maritime communities of the southern Philippines, such as the Tausug on Jolo and the Samal and Tausug on Tawi-tawi, and possibly among other ethnic groups, particularly in and around the southern parts of Mindanao, as well. Among the Tausug, the cultural sanctioning consisted – and probably still consists – of the association of maritime violence, including piracy and coastal raiding, with highly regarded male virtues, such as honour, bravery, magnamity and masculinity. Whereas pecuniary motives were also important, the high status attributed to piratical activity, especially among young men, thus contributed to encouraging the practice. In addition, the raiding activities of previous generations were probably still alive in the historical memory of the Tausug and other communities, further contributing to the cultural sanctioning of piratical activities.

One crucial factor underlies the surge in piracy in all parts of Southeast Asia from the mid-twentieth century, and that is opportunity. In the Sulu region opportunity arose with the motorisation of maritime traffic due to the availability of United States military surplus engines in the aftermath of World War II combined with the proliferation of firearms, both of which greatly facilitated the undertaking of piratical raids and expanded the number of possible targets, both at sea and on far-away coasts. In the Gulf of Thailand, the opportunity consisted of the constant flow of vulnerable prey as thousands of barely seaworthy boats with mostly unarmed and defenceless refugees carrying large sums of cash, jewellery, gold and other valuables, tried to make their way across the Gulf from southern Vietnam to Thailand. In other areas, including the Straits of Malacca and Singapore, the South China Sea and along the major shipping lanes of Indonesia, opportunity arose in part as a consequence of the greater availability of powerful and inexpensive outboard engines from the 1970s, and in part because the crews of international commercial vessels, from around the same time, were heavily reduced, leaving ships much more vulnerable to piratical raids.

Another factor that has enhanced the opportunity for piracy in the region, whether in historic or contemporary times, is migration. In northeast Borneo, piracy and coastal raiding in the post-colonial period was to some extent triggered by the temporary migration of Filipino workers to the British (and later Malaysian) territory. More recently, the Riau pirates who since the early 1980s have attacked commercial vessels in and around the Singapore Strait and the southern parts of the Malacca Strait all seem to be migrants from other parts of Indonesia, and some of them had apparently worked on international commercial vessels before taking to piracy. This suggests that new patterns of migration in the second half of the twentieth century – chiefly labour migration ultimately triggered by the forces of capitalist globalisation – created maritime frontier regions where weak social and political control fed new opportunities for piracy and other forms of criminal activities in the maritime domain. Such opportunities had not existed since the colonial powers in the second half of the nineteenth century had suppressed most piratical activity in the region and dispersed and established control over the communities – such as the sea nomads – that engaged in such practices.

Opportunistic piracy – that is, generally hit-and-run raids perpetrated by small local gangs of pirates with little access to sophisticated equipment or information beforehand – has all along made up the bulk of contemporary piratical activity in Southeast Asia. Organised crime, however, has both thrived on and fed back into opportunistic piracy. In the Gulf of Thailand the attacks against the Vietnamese boat refugees seem mainly to have been perpetrated by opportunistic Thai fishermen-turned-pirates, but there were also indications that more organised and ruthless professional criminals were involved in some of the attacks. Indicating such involvement were both the use of specially designed speedboats and automatic, high velocity firearms to attack the refugees. The reports that several of the abducted Vietnamese girls and women ended up in brothels in Bangkok and other places in Thailand also indicate that the piratical activity was linked to organised criminal groups.

In other places around Southeast Asia, international syndicates – some of which apparently had been involved in other forms of maritime criminal activities, including insurance fraud, documentary fraud and cargo diversion, in the 1960s and 1970s – turned to hijackings of commercial vessels from around the mid-1980s. Whereas hijackings to order were the specialty and main line of activity of some of the smaller organised groups, such as that of Emilio Chengco in the Philippines, for other apparently more organised groups it was mainly a means to procure vessels that could be provided with a phantom identity and used for other, more profitable criminal activities, including cargo diversion and human smuggling.

A third major form of organised piratical activity in Southeast Asia, which surged from around 2000, was the raiding, extortion and kidnapping perpetrated by ostensibly religiously motivated insurgent groups, particularly the Abu Sayyaf Group based in the Sulu Archipelago of the southern Philippines. In spite of the publicity given to the group's purported religious and political objectives, and its links to international terrorist networks, the Abu Sayyaf – or at least its main faction under Khadaffy Janjalani – has since the end of the 1990s moved to become essentially an organised criminal group. Maritime violence, or the threat of violence, is used for economic rather than political purposes and the money thus generated is reinvested in the group's criminal activities and used particularly for buying weapons and attracting more followers. The adherence to Islam, in this context, seems mainly to provide a measure of coherence to the group as well as a sanctioning for its criminal activities.

Even though the distinction between organised and opportunistic piracy is useful in many respects, it should not be allowed to obscure the links that exist between the two types of piracy and between their perpetrators. For example, 'opportunistic' outlaws are attracted to the Abu Sayyaf Group because of its success in undertaking daring and well-planned armed raids and pirate attacks. Some of the opportunistic Thai fishermen-turned-pirates in the late 1970s and 1980s probably collaborated with organised criminals in preying on the boat people or in the trafficking of the victims to prostitution. Opportunistic pirates seem all along to have been hired by international syndicates to carry out well-planned hijackings. The recent spate of hijackings of tugs and barges in the southern Malacca Strait region seems to be organised in even more sophisticated ways whereby local pirates are hired on a contractual basis to take over a particular vessel and then are replaced by another crew. In this way the opportunistic pirates, who only need to have a minimum of information about their employer, can substantially increase their earnings – thereby compensating for the declining returns from low-level armed robberies due to the smaller amounts of cash carried by most commercial vessels today – whereas the syndicates minimise the risk of their organisation being unravelled should the pirates be arrested. The relationship between the opportunistic local pirates in the southern Malacca Strait region and the syndicates thus seems to be symbiotic rather than competitive, thereby perpetuating piracy in the region and adapting it to changing external circumstances.

It remains to be explained why piracy has not yet been efficiently suppressed, in spite of the serious efforts made since the 1980s by various concerned actors, including the authorities of the littoral states in the region, the IMO, the international shipping community and non-government organisations such as the International Maritime

Bureau. Certainly, some measures have contributed to restricting piratical activity, although it may be difficult to appreciate the precise impact of each individual measure. Many attacks have been averted by vigilant crews detecting and preventing pirates from boarding their vessel, and the recent regulations, adopted by the IMO in 2002, that require most international commercial vessels to be equipped with an Automatic Identification System (AIS) and the permanent and prominent display of the ship's identification number, have reduced the opportunity for pirates to hijack vessels. Several of the perpetrators have been arrested over the years by the police and other law enforcement authorities in the region, as well as in China and India, and subsequently sentenced to prison terms of varying length or, in the case of China, capital punishment. Efforts have been made, both on the part of the authorities in the region and on the part of extra-regional powers – mainly Japan and the United States – to enhance the capacity and frequency of naval patrols and surveillance. The problem of piracy has also been extensively discussed in the IMO's Maritime Safety Committee, and representatives of the international shipping industry have taken several initiatives to curb the problem, involving both efforts to put pressure on the governments concerned, and the launching in 1992 of a non-government Piracy Reporting Centre, operated by the IMB, a unit of the International Chamber of Commerce, the main task of which is to collect and publish information about pirate attacks and to assist the law enforcement authorities and the victims of pirate attacks.

Fundamentally, however, in spite of these and other measures, piracy persists because it is not a very big problem for those actors – the governments of the littoral states in the region and the international shipping community – who are in the best position to do something about it, and because they disagree about who should bear the cost of policing the international shipping lanes. For the shipping industry as a whole, the cost of piracy – probably somewhere in the range of US$ 70–200 million per year worldwide – is negligible, and the incentive to make substantial improvements in the security on board ships, for example by installing electric fences or other technical equipment to deter attackers, is relatively small. Moreover, the greater share of the total cost of piracy for the shipping industry is due to a relatively small number of hijackings – today mainly of locally owned and managed tugs and barges – whereas in numbers, most attacks that befall international commercial vessels are low-level armed robberies, the combined cost of which is even more negligible – probably only a few million dollars annually. These attacks rarely involve the killing or injuring of crew members, and shipping companies often refrain from reporting such attacks to the local authorities for fear that the cost of delays in connection with police investigations be more costly than the value of money, stores and valuables stolen. Similarly, shipowners are also reluctant to report attacks that involve the kidnapping-for-ransom of crew members for fear that doing so may jeopardise the lives and well-being of the hostages.

As a consequence, local law enforcement authorities often lack reports of incidents that have occurred in or around their territorial waters, or the information is only conveyed after a considerable delay of several days or even weeks. However, whereas not reporting a low-level armed robbery to the authorities may make sense in the short term for the individual shipmaster and shipping company, the accumulated long-term effect of not doing so is to hamper the efforts of the authorities to deal with the problem. The problem is further exacerbated by the reluctance of many crew members to testify in local courts and, sometimes, by the shipowners' reluctance to bear the costs of travel and other expenses for the witnesses to be able to give their testimonies.

To the extent that the shipping and insurance industries have contributed financially to the efforts to suppress piracy, this has mainly been in the form of voluntary contributions to the IMB's Piracy Reporting Centre, the operation of which since 1992 has greatly improved reporting and information sharing about piracy in Southeast Asia as well as in the rest of the world. However, the industry, together with most of the international maritime community, with the exception of Japan, has ignored calls by Indonesia and Malaysia for a cost-sharing arrangement to finance the policing of the Malacca Strait against pirates. From the point of view of the littoral states it seems reasonable if such costs were borne not only by the countries bordering the Strait but also by those using it for various purposes.

Indonesia and the Philippines, in particular, with their overstretched navies and other marine law enforcement authorities, are unable efficiently to police their vast territorial waters and exclusive economic zones, and in the more comprehensive context of their maritime security, piracy is of relatively small importance. Several other problems linked to the maritime domain are of greater priority, both in terms of state and human security. These problems include illegal fishing by foreign trawlers, bomb fishing and other threats to the maritime environment, smuggling of humans, drugs and other illicit goods including arms, armed insurgencies and, possibly, the threat of maritime terrorism. Tackling these issues from a regional point of view involves a number of sensitivities over national sovereignty that are unlikely to be solved in the near future.

The weakness of the navies and law enforcement authorities of the littoral states in Southeast Asia, particularly Indonesia and the Philippines, combined with the relatively low priority given to the problem of piracy by those countries thus explains why the efforts to suppress piracy so far only have had limited effect. Of the countries in maritime Southeast Asia, only Singapore regards piracy as a matter of great urgency, especially since the problem, in the wake of the events of 11 September 2001, has come largely to be treated in conjunction with the potential threat of a maritime terrorist attack against the city state or its economic interests. As for the other Southeast Asian states, forceful measures against the problem of piracy have mainly been taken after international pressure, such as when Indonesia in 1992 cracked down on the pirates operating out of Riau and launched joint naval patrols with Singapore and Malaysia, or when the MALSINDO patrols were announced in mid-2004 after the United States earlier the same year had presented its Regional Maritime Security Initiative (RMSI), which looked set to give a leading role to the United States in a future maritime security regime. However, even though such efforts may have been successful in the short term, the ensuing decreases in piratical activity have generally not been sustained because the main aim of the efforts has been to diffuse international criticism or avert the threat of foreign intervention in the region – not to eradicate piracy in the region once and for all.

An end to the problem of piracy in maritime Southeast Asia will demand the full commitment of the governments of all major countries in the region, and such a commitment will only come about if the suppression of piracy is seen as an important security objective. Presently, a range of other issues in the maritime domain, including illegal fishing, smuggling and environmental degradation, are of more immediate concern to most countries in maritime Southeast Asia, particularly those with the greatest archipelagic waters. Several of these issues, moreover, highlight contradictory interests between the states involved as well as sensitivities over matters concerning national sovereignty. In this context, the best chance for an enduring solution to the problem of piracy is if it can be integrated into a regional, multinational maritime security regime that takes its point of departure in the concerns of the Southeast Asian nations and takes account both of the need for maritime security for the international shipping community and other international users of Southeast Asia's waterways and of the social, economic and political interests of the region's human population.

Bibliography

Archival Sources

Algemeen Rijksarchief (ARA), The Hague

Ministerie van buitenlandse zaken, juridische en andere zaken (MvBZ), A-dossiers.

International Maritime Organization (IMO), London

[Records of the] Assembly (A).

[Records of the] Maritime Safety Committee (MSC).

Maritime Safety Committee Circulars (MSC/Circ.).*

National Archives (NA), Public Records Office, Kew (London)

Records created or inherited by the Air Ministry, the Royal Air Force, and related bodies, 1862–1992 (AIR).

Records of the Colonial Office, Commonwealth and Foreign and Commonwealth Offices, Empire Marketing Board, and related bodies, 1570–1990 (CO).

Records created or inherited by the Dominions Office, and of the Commonwealth Relations and Foreign and Commonwealth Offices, 1843–1990 (DO).

Records created and inherited by the Foreign Office, 1567–2003 (FO).

Records created or inherited by the War Office, Armed Forces, Judge Advocate General, and related bodies, 1568–1996 (WO).

United Nations (UN), Lund University Library Collection, Lund

[Records of the] General Assembly (A).

---

* Some of the cited MSC Circulars from the period 2000–2005 are available from the IMO's web page at http://www.imo.org/home.asp, accessed on 10 October 2005.

Other Unpublished Sources and Reports

ICC (International Chamber of Commerce) – International Maritime Bureau, Barking, Essex.

—— (1983) 'International terrorism: The threat to shipping. A Special Report by the ICC International Maritime Bureau'.

—— (1985) 'A third report into the incidence of piracy and armed robbery from merchant ships'.

—— (1992a) 'Special Report Piracy'.

—— (1992b) 'Piratical Attacks in 1992'.

—— (1993) 'Piracy Report (1st January–31st December 1993) from the IMB – Regional Piracy Centre'.

—— (1994a) 'Piracy Update (1st January–30th June 1994) from the IMB – Regional Piracy Centre'.

—— (1994b) 'Piracy Report (1st January–31st December 1993) from the IMB – Regional Piracy Centre'.

—— (1995) 'Piracy Report (1st January – 31st December 1994) from the IMB – Regional Piracy Centre, Kuala Lumpur'.

—— (1996) 'Piracy: Annual Report (1st January–31st December 1995) compiled by IMB Regional Piracy Centre, Kuala Lumpur'.

—— (1997) 'Piracy: Annual Report (1st January–31st December 1996): IMB Regional Piracy Centre, Kuala Lumpur'.

—— (1998a) 'Piracy and Armed Robbery against Ships: Annual Report 1st January–31st December 1997'.

—— (1998b) 'Piracy and Armed Robbery Against Ships: A special report. Revised edition – March 1998'.

—— (1999) 'Piracy and Armed Robbery against Ships: Annual Report 1st January–31st December 1998'.

—— (2000) 'Piracy and Armed Robbery against Ships: Annual Report 1st January–31st December 1999'.

—— (2001) 'Piracy and Armed Robbery against Ships: Annual Report 1st January–31st December 2000'.

—— (2002) 'Piracy and Armed Robbery against Ships: Annual Report 1st January–31st December 2001'.

—— (2003) 'Piracy and Armed Robbery against Ships: Annual Report 1st January–31st December 2002'.

—— (2004) 'Piracy and Armed Robbery against Ships: Annual Report 1st January–31st December 2003'.

—— (2005a) 'Piracy and Armed Robbery against Ships: Annual Report 1st January–31st December 2004'.

—— (2005b) 'Piracy and Armed Robbery against Ships. Report for the period 1 January – 30 September 2005'.

International Crime Threat Assessment (2000) 'International Crime Threat Assessment', available at the Internet web page http://www.fas.org/irp/threat/pub45270index.html, accessed on 7 July 2004.

International Crisis Group (2004) 'Southern Philippines Backgrounder: Terrorism and the Peace Process', ICG Asia Report no. 80.

Ministry of Home Affairs of the Government of Singapore (2003) 'White Paper: The Jemaah Islamiyah Arrests and the Threat of Terrorism'.

NUMAST (undated) 'In the firing line: A NUMAST report on the threat to merchant shipping posed by piracy, armed robbery and terrorism'.

Organization for Economic Co-operation and Development (2003) 'Security in Maritime Transport: Risk Factors and Economic Impact'.

Sutedjo (1992) 'Workable Operational Structures to Combat Piracy Activities in the Region', unpublished paper presented at the conference on 'Piracy in Southeast Asia', Kuala Lumpur, 28–29 July 1992.

United States Department of State (2004) 'Patterns of Global Terrorism 2003', available at the Internet web page http://www.state.gov/documents/organization/31946.pdf, accessed on 17 November 2004.

Published Sources

Books and Manuals

Bastin, John and Robin W. Winks (eds) (1966) *Malaysia: Selected Historical Readings*, Kuala Lumpur, London, New York and Melbourne: Oxford University Press.

BIMCO (1998) *The ShipMaster's Security Manual*, Copenhagen: BIMCO.

Blyth, Ken (2000) *Petro Pirates: The Hijacking of the Petro Ranger*, St Leonards, NSW: Allen & Unwin.

Committee on Foreign Affairs, House of Representatives (1982) *Hearing before the Subcommittee on Asian and Pacific Affairs of the Committee on Foreign Affairs, House of Representatives, Ninety-seventh Congress, Second Session, April 29, 1982*, Washington, DC: U.S. Government Printing Office.

Fa-hsien (1956) *The Travels of Fa-hsien (399–414 A.D.), or Record of the Buddhistic Kingdoms. Re-translated by H. A. Giles, M.A.*, London: Routledge and Kegan Paul.

International Chamber of Shipping and International Shipping Federation (2004) *Pirates and Armed Robbers: Guidelines on Prevention for Masters and Ship Security Officers*, 4th edition, London: Marisec.

Nhat Tien, Duong Phuc and Vu Thanh Thuy (1981) *Pirates on the Gulf of Siam: Report from the Vietnamese Boat People Living in the Refugee Camp in Songkhla – Thailand*, 2nd edition, San Diego, CA: Boat People S.O.S. Committee.

Norwegian Shipowners' Association (1997) *Piracy: Armed Robbery from Ships*, Oslo: Norwegian Shipowners' Association.

Truong Nhu Tang (1986) *A Vietcong Memoir*, New York: Vintage Books.

Print Media

Angkatan Bersenjata. Jakarta, daily.

Asiaweek. Hong Kong, weekly.

Berita Harian. Jakarta, daily.

Daily Telegraph. London, daily.

The Economist. London, weekly.

Far Eastern Economic Review. Hong Kong, weekly.

Forbes. New York, biweekly.

Jakarta Post. Jakarta, daily.

Kompas. Jakarta, daily.

Latitudes. Denpasar, monthly.

Media Indonesia. Jakarta, daily.

Merdeka. Jakarta, daily.

New Straits Times. Kuala Lumpur, daily.

New York Times. New York, daily.

Republika. Jakarta, daily.

Sijori Pos. Nagoya (Batam), daily.

Sinar Harapan. Jakarta, daily.

The Star. Kuala Lumpur, daily.

Straits Times. Singapore, daily.

Straits Times Weekly Overseas Edition. Singapore, weekly.

Suara Karya. Jakarta, daily.

Suara Pembaruan. Jakarta, daily.

SundayStar. Kuala Lumpur, weekly.

Tempo. Jakarta, weekly.

Time (Asian edition). Hong Kong, weekly.

Wall Street Journal (Eastern edition). Hong Kong, daily.

Washington Post. Washington D.C., daily.

Electronic Media and New Agencies

Agence France Presse, http://www.afp.com/home/

Antara, http://www.antara.co.id/

Dépeche EDA (Eglise d'Asie) (Internet edition), http://eglasie.mepasie.org

Global Nation, http://www.inq7.net/globalnation

ICC (International Chamber of Commerce) News Archives, http://www.iccwbo.org/display2/index.html

Manila Standard Today (Internet edition), http://www.manilastandardtoday.com/?page=index

Manila Times (Internet edition), http://www.manilatimes.net/

Penguin Star, http://www.geocities.com/Yosemite/7915/HomePage.html

Sun Star (Internet edition), http://www.sunstar.com.ph/

Sydney Morning Herald (Internet edition), http://www.smh.com.au/

The Telegraph (Internet edition), http://www.telegraph.co.uk

Tempo Interaktif, http://www.tempointeraktif.com/

Time (Asian Internet edition), http://www.time.com/time/asia/

LITERATURE

Abhyankar, Jayant (2001) 'Maritime Fraud and Piracy', in Phil Williams and Dimitri Vlassis (eds) *Combating Transnational Crime: Concepts, Activities and Responses*, London and Portland, OR: Frank Cass, pp. 157–194.

—— (2002) 'Piracy and Maritime Violence: A Continuing Threat to Maritime Industry', unpublished paper, available at the web page http://www.itopf.com/Abhyankar.pdf, accessed on 27 May 2004.

Ahmad, Hamzah (1997) 'The Straits of Malacca: A Profile', in Hamzah Ahmad (ed.) *The Straits of Malacca: International Co-operation in Trade, Funding and Navigational Safety*, Kuala Lumpur: Pelanduk and Maritime Institute of Malaysia.

Andaya, Barbara Watson and Leonard Y. Andaya (2001) *A History of Malaysia*, 2nd edition, Houndmills, Basingstoke: Palgrave.

Aschan, Jan (1996) 'Pirater i paradiset', in *Årsbok om Kina*, Malmö: Svensk-kinesiska föreningen, pp. 46–50.

Beckman, Robert C. (2002) 'Combating Piracy and Armed Robbery against Ships in Southeast Asia: The Way Forward', *Ocean Development and International Law*, vol. 33, pp. 317–341.

Beckman, Robert C., Carl Grundy-Warr and Vivian L. Forbes (1994) 'Acts of Piracy in the Malacca and Singapore Straits', *Maritime Briefing (International Boundaries Research Unit)*, vol. 1, no. 4.

Blaney III, Harry C. (1989) 'Anti-Piracy in South-East Asia: US and International Efforts and Programmes', in Eric Ellen (ed.) *Piracy at Sea*, Paris: ICC Publishing, pp. 101–106.

Blumentritt, Ferd (1882) 'Versuch einer Ethnographie der Philippinen', Erganzungsheft No. 67 zu *Dr A. Petermann's Mittheilungen aus Justus Perthes' geographischer Anstalt*, Band 28, Gotha: Justus Perthes.

Boulanger, Pascal (1989) 'The Gulf of Thailand', in Eric Ellen (ed.) *Piracy at Sea*, Paris: ICC Publishing, pp. 83–96.

Boxer, Charles Ralph (1985) *Portuguese Conquest and Commerce in Southern Asia, 1500–1750*, London: Variorum Reprints.

Bradford, John F. (2004) 'Japanese Anti-Piracy Initiatives in Southeast Asia: Policy Formulation and the Coastal State Responses', *Contemporary Southeast Asia*, vol. 26, no. 3, pp. 480–505.

—— (2005) 'The Growing Prospects for Maritime Security Cooperation in Southeast Asia', *Naval College Review*, vol. 58, no. 3.

Burnett, John S. (2002) *Dangerous Waters: Modern Piracy and Terror on the High Seas*, New York: Dutton.

Butcher, John G. (2004) *The Closing of the Frontier: A History of the Marine Fisheries of Southeast Asia c. 1850–2000*, Singapore: Institute of Southeast Asian Studies.

Buzan, Barry, Ole Wæver and Jaap de Wilde (1998) *Security: A New Framework for Analysis*, Boulder, CO: Lynne Rienner.

Capie, David (2002) *Small Arms Production and Transfers in Southeast Asia*, Canberra Papers on Strategy and Defence No. 146, Canberra: Strategic and Defence Studies Centre, Australian National University.

Carpenter, William M. and David G. Wiencek (2000) *Asian Security Handbook 2000*, Armonk, NY: M.E. Sharpe.

Chalk, Peter (1998) 'Contemporary Maritime Piracy in Southeast Asia', *Studies in Conflict & Terrorism*, vol. 21, pp. 87–112.

—— (2000) *Non-military Security and Global Order: the Impact of Extremism, Violence and Chaos on National and International Security*, New York: St. Martin's Press.

—— (2002) 'Militant Islamic Extremism in the Southern Philippines', in Jason F. Isaacson and Colin Rubenstein (eds), *Islam in Asia: Changing Political Realities*, New Brunswick, NJ, and London: Transaction Publishers, pp. 187–222.

Chong Chee Kin (2000) 'Attack is no surprise for Semporna folk', unpublished article available at http://www.malaysia.net/lists/sangkancil/2000-04/msg01132.html, accessed on 21 May 2004.

Coady, C. A. J. (2004) 'Terrorism and Innocence', *The Journal of Ethics*, vol. 8, pp. 37–58.

Collins, Alan (2003) *Security and Southeast Asia: Domestic, Regional, and Global Issues*, Singapore: Institute of Southeast Asian Studies.

Committee on the Effect of Smaller Crews on Maritime Safety (1990) *Crew Size and Maritime Safety*, Washington, DC: National Academy Press.

Cribb, Robert (2000) *Historical Atlas of Indonesia*, Honolulu: University of Hawai'i Press.

Djalal, Hasjim (2005) 'Combating Piracy: Co-operation Needs, Efforts and Challenges', in Derek Johnson and Mark Valencia (eds), *Piracy in Southeast Asia: Status, Issues, and Responses*, Leiden and Singapore: International Institute for Asian Studies and Institute of Southeast Asian Studies, pp. 143–159.

Donnelly, Charles (2004) 'Terrorism in the Southern Philippines: Contextualising the Abu Sayyaf Group as an Islamist Secessionist Organisation', paper for the 15th Biennial Conference of the Asian Studies Association of Australia, Canberra, 29 June–2 July 2004.

Dragonette, Charles N. (2005) 'Lost at Sea', *Foreign Affairs*, vol 84, no. 2, pp. 174–175.

Dupont, Pascal (1986) *Pirates d'aujourd'hui*, Paris: Editions Ramsay.

Economist Intelligence Unit (1992a) *Indonesia Country Report No 3 1992.*

—— (1992b) *Indonesia Country Report No 4 1992.*

Eklöf, Stefan (2005), 'The Return of Piracy: Decolonization and International Relations in a Maritime Border Region (the Sulu Sea), 1959–63', Working Paper No. 15, Centre for East and South-East Asian Studies, Lund University.

—— (forthcoming) 'Contemporary Southeast Asian Piracy in Global Perspective', in Terence Chong (ed.), *Globalization and Its Counterforces: Aspects from East and Southeast Asia*, Singapore: Institute of Southeast Asian Studies.

Ellen, Eric (1992) 'A Look into Asian Piracy', *Asian Defence Journal*, no 9, pp. 19–22.

—— (ed.) (1989) *Piracy at Sea*, Paris: ICC Publishing.

Emmers, Ralf (2003) 'ASEAN and the Securitization of Transnational Crime in Southeast Asia', *The Pacific Review*, vol. 16, no. 3, pp. 419–438.

—— (2004), *Non-traditional Security in the Asia-Pacific: The Dynamics of Securitisation*, Singapore: Eastern University Press.

Fewsmith, Joseph (1999) 'China in 1998: Tacking to Stay the Course', *Asian Survey*, vol. 39, no. 1, pp. 99–113.

Frake, Charles O. (1998) 'Abu Sayyaf Displays of Violence and the Proliferation of Contested Identities among Philippine Muslims', *American Anthropologist*, vol. 100, no. 1, pp. 41–54.

Frécon, Eric (2002) *Pavillon noir sur l'Asie du Sud-Est: Histoire d'une résurgence de la piraterie maritime*, Paris and Bangkok: L'Harmattan and IRASEC (Institut de Recherche sur l'Asie du Sud Est Contemporaine).

—— (2006) 'Piracy and Armed Robbery at Sea in Southeast Asia: Initial Impressions from the Field', in Graham Gerard Ong (ed.), *Piracy, Maritime Terrorism and Securing Maritime Southeast Asia*, Singapore: Institute of Southeast Asian Studies (forthcoming).

Gottschalk, Jack A. and Brian P. Flanagan (2000) *Jolly Roger with an Uzi: The Rise and Threat of Modern Piracy*, Annapolis, MD: Naval Institute Press.

Gutierrez, Eric (2000) 'New Faces of Violence in Muslim Mindanao', in Kristina Gaerlan and Mara Stankovitch (eds) *Rebels, Warlords and Ulama: A Reader on Muslim Separatism and the War in Southern Philippines*, Quezon City: Institute for Popular Democracy.

Hall, Kenneth R. (1985) *Maritime Trade and State Development in Early Southeast Asia*, Honolulu: University of Hawai'i Press.

Hedman, Eva-Lotta and John T. Sidel (2000) *Philippine Politics and Society in the Twentieth Century: Colonial legacies, post-colonial trajectories*, London and New York: Routledge.

Henkel, Joachim (1989) 'Refugees on the High Seas: A Dangerous Passage', in Eric Ellen (ed.), *Piracy at Sea*, Paris: ICC Publishing, pp. 107–112.

Hurley, Vic (1997 [1936]) *Swish of the Kris*. Republished as e-book at the Internet web page http://www.bakbakan.com/swishkb.html, accessed on 21 June 2005.

Hyslop, I. R. (1989) 'Contemporary Piracy', in Eric Ellen (ed.), *Piracy at Sea*, Paris: ICC Publishing, pp. 3–40.

Kasemsri, Bhirabongse (1989) 'The Situation of Refugees in the Territorial Waters of Thailand', in Eric Ellen (ed.) *Piracy at Sea*, Paris: ICC Publishing, pp. 113–117.

Kiefer, Thomas M. (1972) *The Tausug: Violence and Law in a Philippine Moslem Society*, New York: Holt, Rinehart and Winston.

Knutsen, Torbjørn L. (1997) *A History of International Relations Theory*, 2nd edition, Manchester and New York: Manchester University Press.

Lindquist, Johan (2002) *The Anxieties of Mobility: Development, Migration, and Tourism in the Indonesian Borderlands*, Stockholm: Department of Social Anthropology, Stockholm University.

Lintner, Bertil (2000) 'The Perils of Rising Piracy', in *Janes Defence Weekly*, 15 November 2000, pp. 18–19.

—— (2003), *Blood Brothers: The Criminal Underworld of Asia*, New York: Palgrave Macmillan.

Liss, Carolin (2003) 'Maritime Piracy in Southeast Asia', *Southeast Asian Affairs 2003*, pp. 52–68.

—— (2005) 'Private Security Companies in the Fight against Piracy in Asia', Working Paper No 120, Perth: Asia Research Centre, Murdoch University.

Lombard, Denys (1979) 'Regard nouveau sur les "pirates Malais" 1ère moitié du XIXe s.', *Archipel*, vol. 18, pp. 231–250.

Lowry, Robert (1996) *The Armed Forces of Indonesia*, St Leonards, NSW: Allen & Unwin.

Luft, Gal and Anne Korin (2004) 'Terrorism Goes to Sea', *Foreign Affairs*, vol. 83, no. 6, pp. 61–71.

Mak Joon Num (2006) 'Unilateralism and Regionalism: Working Together and Alone in the Malacca Straits', in Graham Gerard Ong (ed.), *Piracy, Maritime Terrorism and Securing Maritime Southeast Asia*, Singapore: Institute of Southeast Asian Studies (forthcoming).

Miller, Harry (1970) *Pirates of the Far East*, London: Robert Hale & Co.

Mukundan, P. (2004) 'Terrorism and Piracy Threats: Scourge of Piracy in Southeast Asia – Any Improvements in 2004?', in *Regional Outlook Forum*, Singapore: Institute of Southeast Asian Studies.

Noble, Lela Garner (1977) *Philippine Policy towards Sabah: A Claim to Independence*, Tucson: University of Arizona Press.

Ong, Graham Gerard (2005) 'Ships Can Be Dangerous Too: Coupling Piracy and Terrorism in Southeast Asia's Maritime Security Framework', in Derek Johnson and Mark Valencia (eds), *Piracy in Southeast Asia: Status, Issues, and Responses*, Leiden and Singapore: International Institute for Asian Studies and Institute of Southeast Asian Studies, pp. 45–76.

—— (ed.) (2006) *Piracy, Maritime Terrorism and Securing Maritime Southeast Asia*, Singapore: Institute of Southeast Asian Studies (forthcoming).

Ormerod, Henry A. (1924) *Piracy in the Ancient World: An Essay in Mediterranean History*, Liverpool and London: Liverpool University Press.

Palma, Mary Ann E. (2003), 'Legal and Political Responses to Maritime Security Challenges in the Straits of Malacca and Singapore', CANCAPS (Canadian Consortium on Asia Pacific Security) Paper Number 31.

Pennell, C. R. (1994) 'Piracy in a Historical and Geographical Context', unpublished paper for the 'Phantom Ships and Piracy Meeting', Kuala Lumpur, 12–20 July 1994.

Pérotin-Dumon, Anne (2001), 'The Pirate and the Emperor: Power and the Law on the Seas, 1450–1850', in C. R. Pennell (ed.), *Bandits at Sea: A*

Pirates Reader, New York and London: New York University Press, pp. 25–54.

Perret, Daniel (1998) 'Notes sur la piraterie moderne en Méditerranée Sud-Est asiatique', *Archipel*, vol. 56: I, pp. 121–144.

Pringle, Robert (1970) *Rajahs and Rebels; The Ibans of Sarawak under Brooke Rule, 1841–1941*, London: Macmillan.

Rediker, Marcus (2004) *Villains of All Nations: Atlantic Pirates in the Golden Age*, London and New York: Verso.

Reid, Anthony (1993) *Southeast Asia in the Age of Commerce 1450–1680. Volume Two: Expansion and Crisis*, New Haven and London: Yale University Press.

Renwick, Neil and Jason Abbott (1999) 'Piratical Violence and Maritime Security in Southeast Asia', *Security Dialogue*, vol. 30, no. 2, pp. 183–196.

Richardson, Michael (2004) *A Time Bomb for Global Trade: Maritime-related Terrorism in an Age of Weapons of Mass Destruction*, Singapore: Institute of Southeast Asian Studies.

Robinson, W. Courtland (1998) *Terms of Refuge: The Indochinese Exodus and the International Response*, London and New York: Zed Books.

Rodger, N. A. M. (2004) *The Safeguard of the Sea: A Naval History of Britain, 660–1649*, London: Penguin.

Rosenthal, Justine A. (2003) 'Southeast Asia: Archipelago of Afghanistans?', *Orbis*, vol. 47, no. 3, pp. 479–493.

Rubin, Alfred P. (1998) *The Law of Piracy*, Irvington-on-Hudson, NY: Transnational Publishers.

Russel, Roth (1981) *Muddy Glory: America's "Indian Wars" in the Philippines, 1899–1935*, W. Hanover, MA: Christopher Publishing House.

Rutter, Owen (1986) *The Pirate Wind: Tales of the Sea-robbers of Malaya*, London: Hutchinson.

Ryter, Loren (1998) 'Pemuda Pancasila: The Last Loyalist Free Men of Suharto's Order?', *Indonesia*, no. 66, pp. 45–73.

Sanger, Clyde (1987) *Ordering the Oceans: The Making of the Law of the Sea*, Toronto and Buffalo: University of Toronto Press.

Santos, Eduardo (2000) 'Anti-Piracy Operations in the Philippines: A Briefing Manuscript for Piracy Briefing', unpublished paper for the 3rd OTW Anti-Piracy Forum International, Tokyo, 24 October 2000.

—— (2004) 'Piracy and Armed Robbery against Ships: Philippine Perspective', unpublished paper for the Workshop on Maritime Security, Maritime Terrorism and Piracy in Asia, organised by the Institute of Southeast Asian Studies (Singapore) and the International Institute of Asian Studies (Leiden), Singapore, 23–24 September 2004.

Sather, Clifford (1997) *The Bajau Laut: Adaption, History, and Fate in a Maritime Fishing Society of South-eastern Sabah*, Kuala Lumpur, Oxford, Singapore and New York: Oxford University Press.

Sazlan, Iskandar. 'Incidents at Sea: Shipjacking, Maritime Muggings and Thefts in Southeast Asia', unpublished paper presented at the Intercargo Roundtable Discussion on Piracy, Singapore, 4 February 2002.

Schulze, Kirsten (2004) *The Free Aceh Movement (GAM): Anatomy of a Separatist Organization*, Policy Studies 2, Washington DC: East–West Center.

Sebastian, Leonard C. (2003) 'The Indonesian Dilemma: How to Participate in the War on Terror without Becoming a National Security State', in Kumar Ramakrishna and See Seng Tan (eds), *After Bali: The Threat of Terrorism in Southeast Asia*, Singapore: World Scientific and Institute of Defense and Strategic Studies and Nanyang Technological University, pp. 357–382.

Sidel, John Thayer (1995) 'Coercion, Capital, and the Post-colonial State: Bossism in the Postwar Philippines', unpub. Ph.D. thesis, Cornell University, N. Y., UMI Dissertation Services, order no. 9511858.

Stuart, Robert (2002) *In Search of Pirates: A Modern-Day Odyssey in the South China Sea*, Edinburgh and London: Mainstream Publishing.

Tagliacozzo, Eric (2000) 'Kettle on a Slow Boil: Batavia's Threat Perceptions in the Indies' Outer Islands, 1870–1910', *Journal of Southeast Asian Studies*, vol. 31, no. 1, pp. 70–100.

Tarling, Nicholas (1978) *Piracy and Politics in the Malay World: A Study of British Imperialism in Nineteenth-century South-East Asia*, Nendeln/Liechtenstein: Kraus Reprint.

Teitler, Ger (2002) 'Piracy in Southeast Asia: A Historical Comparison', *MAST (Maritime Studies)*, vol. 1, no. 1, pp. 67–83.

Tregonning, Kennedy Gordon (1965) *A History of Modern Sabah (North Borneo 1881–1963)*, 2nd edition, London, New York and Toronto: Oxford University Press.

Trocki, Carl A. (1979) *Prince of Pirates: The Temenggongs and the Development of Johor and Singapore, 1784–1885*, Singapore: Singapore University Press.

United Nations High Commissioner for Refugees (2000) *The State of the World's Refugees: Fifty Years of Humanitarian Action*, Oxford: Oxford University Press.

Vagg, Jon (1995) 'Rough Seas? Contemporary Piracy in South East Asia', *British Journal of Criminology*, vol. 35, no. 1, pp. 63–80.

Valencia, Mark (2005a) 'Piracy and Terrorism in Southeast Asia: Similarities, Differences, and Their Implications', in Derek Johnson and

Mark Valencia (eds), *Piracy in Southeast Asia: Status, Issues, and Responses*, Leiden and Singapore: International Institute for Asian Studies and Institute of Southeast Asian Studies, pp. 77–102.

—— (2005b) 'Piracy and Politics in Southeast Asia', in Derek Johnson and Mark Valencia (eds), *Piracy in Southeast Asia: Status, Issues, and Responses*, Leiden and Singapore: International Institute for Asian Studies and Institute of Southeast Asian Studies, pp. 103–121.

van de Bunt, H. G. and E. K. J. Pladdet (2003) 'Geweld op zee: Een verkenning naar de aard en omvang van zeepiraterij', *Justitiële verkenningen*, no. 2, pp. 29–43.

Villar, Roger (1985) *Piracy Today: Robbery and Violence at Sea since 1980*, London: Conway Maritime Press.

Warren, James Francis (1981) *The Sulu Zone 1768–1898: The Dynamics of External Trade, Slavery, and Ethnicity in the Transformation of a Southeast Asian Maritime State*, Singapore: Singapore University Press.

—— (2002) *Iranun and Balangingi: Globalization, Maritime Raiding and the Birth of Ethnicity*, Singapore: Singapore University Press.

—— (2003) *A Tale of Two Centuries: The Globalisation of Maritime Raiding and Piracy in Southeast Asia at the End of the Eighteenth and Twentieth Centuries*, Working Paper Series, No. 2, Singapore: Asia Research Institute, National University of Singapore.

Wheatley, Paul (1961) *The Golden Khersonese: Studies in the Historical Geography of the Malay Peninsula before A. D. 1500*, Kuala Lumpur: University of Malaya Press.

Williams M. G., Clive (2003) 'The Question of "Links" between Al Qaeda and Southeast Asia', in Kumar Ramarkrishna and See Seng Tan (eds), *After Bali: The Threat of Terrrorism in Southeast Asia*, Singapore: World Scientific, Institute of Defense and Strategic Studies and Nanyang Technological University, pp. 83–95.

Wolters, O. W. (1967) *Early Indonesian Commerce: A Study of the Origins of Srivijaya*, Ithaca, NY: Cornell University Press.

Young, Adam J. (2005) 'Roots of Contemporary Maritime Piracy in Southeast Asia', in Derek Johnson and Mark Valencia (eds), *Piracy in Southeast Asia: Status, Issues, and Responses*, Leiden and Singapore: International Institute for Asian Studies and Institute of Southeast Asian Studies, pp. 1–33.

Young, Adam J. and Mark Valencia (2003) 'Conflation of Piracy and Terrorism in Southeast Asia: Rectitude and Utility', *Contemporary Southeast Asia*, vol. 25, no. 2, pp. 269–283.

Index